The Ultimate Ninja Foodi Pressure Cooker Cookbook

800+ Easy, Healthy and Delicious Recipes to Pressure Cook, Air Fry, Dehydrate, Slow Cook, and more

Amy Boggs

© **Copyright 2020 - All rights reserved.**

The content contained within this book may not be reproduced, duplicated or transmitted without direct written permission from the author or the publisher.

Under no circumstances will any blame or legal responsibility be held against the publisher, or author, for any damages, reparation, or monetary loss due to the information contained within this book, either directly or indirectly.

Legal Notice:
This book is copyright protected. It is only for personal use. You cannot amend, distribute, sell, use, quote or paraphrase any part, or the content within this book, without the consent of the author or publisher.

Disclaimer Notice:
Please note the information contained within this document is for educational and entertainment purposes only. All effort has been executed to present accurate, up to date, reliable, complete information. No warranties of any kind are declared or implied. Readers acknowledge that the author is not engaged in the rendering of legal, financial, medical or professional advice. The content within this book has been derived from various sources. Please consult a licensed professional before attempting any techniques outlined in this book.

By reading this document, the reader agrees that under no circumstances is the author responsible for any losses, direct or indirect, that are incurred as a result of the use of the information contained within this document, including, but not limited to, errors, omissions, or inaccuracies.

Table of Contents

Introduction 7

Chapter 1: Breakfast Recipes 8

    Classical Fried Eggs 8

    Cheese Casserole 8

    Jalapeno Chicken Wings 8

    Asparagus Frittata 8

    Curry Shredded Chicken 9

    Parmesan Chicken Wings 9

    Green Beans Omelet 9

    Low Carb Morning Casserole 10

    Eggs in Bacon Cups 10

    Asparagus and Bacon Plate 10

    Chili Chicken Bites 10

    Feta Frittata 11

    Fish with Sesame 11

    Hard Boiled Eggs with Bacon Filling 11

    Western Omelet 12

    Keto Cheddar Bites 12

    Keto Juicy Bacon Strips 12

    Chorizo Fritatta 12

    Breakfast Pork Chops 13

    Quiche Lorraine 13

    Chicken Sandwiches 13

    Breakfast Muffins 14

    Bacon Jalapeno 14

    Eggs in Mushroom Hats 14

    Butter Chicken Bites 14

Chapter 2: Beef, Lamb and Pork Recipes 16

    Delicious Braised Pork Neck Bones 16

    Pot Roast 16

    Beef Chili & Cornbread Casserole 17

    Macaroni and Cheese 17

    Easy Sausage and Peppers 17

    Chinese Style Beef 18

    Easy Short Ribs and Root Vegetables 18

    Beef and Spinach 19

    Beef Soup 19

    Tex-Mex Meatloaf Recipe 19

    Delicious Beef Recipe 20

    Sausage and Chard Pasta Sauce 20

    Pork Shoulder Chops with Carrots 20

    BBQ Pulled Beef Sandwiches 21

    Mouthwatering Beef Stew 21

    Herbed Beef 22

    Oregano Meatballs 22

    Beef Roast 22

    Chinese Pork 22

    Delicious Pulled Pork Sandwiches 22

    Honey Mustard Pork Tenderloin Recipe 23

    Classic Brisket with Veggies 23

    BBQ Pork with Ginger Coconut and Sweet Potatoes 24

    Delightful Lamb Shanks with Pancetta 24

    Cinnamon Pork 25

    Special Biscuits 25

    Lamb and Eggplant Casserole 26

    Pork Loin and Apples 26

Beef Bites 27

Paprika Pork Chops 27

Pork Carnitas 27

Pork Meatballs 27

Smoked Pork 27

Pork Chops 28

Amazing Pork Chops with Applesauce 28

Simple Spare Ribs with Wine 29

Yummy Pork Chops 29

Garlic Pork Chops 29

Ninja Pulled Pork 29

Rosemary Sausage and Onion 30

Peppers and Pork Stew 30

Buttery Pork Steaks 31

Garlic Pork 31

Chapter 3: Poultry Recipes 32

Best Butter Chicken 32

Cheesy Chicken and Bacon Chowder 32

Chicken and Chimichuri 32

Herbed Whole Roasted Chicken 33

Turkey Breast 33

Great Chicken Wings 34

Black Bean Soup 34

Chicken and cashews 34

Best BBQ and Honey Glazed Wings 35

Rosemary Turkey 35

Stuffed Chicken Recipe 35

Easy Chicken Teriyaki 36

Vegetable Stock Recipe 36

Creamy Asparagus Soup 36

Chicken and Tomatoes 37

Chicken Stock Recipe 37

Cumin Chicken Wings 37

Rotisserie Chicken 38

Chapter 4: Fish and Seafood Recipes 39

Fish & Fries 39

Crispy Shrimp 39

Southern Fried Fish Fillet 39

Ranch Fish Fillet 40

Ranch Warm Fillets 40

Tuna Patties 40

Crispy Cod Fish 41

Breathtaking Cod Fillets 41

Fish & Chips with Herb Sauce 41

Fish Sticks 42

Salmon Paprika 42

Garlic and Lemon Prawn Delight 42

Paprika Salmon 43

Kale and Salmon Delight 43

Coconut Shrimp 43

Crispy Fish Nuggets 44

Adventurous Sweet and Sour Fish 44

Lovely Carb Soup 44

Heartfelt Sesame Fish 44

Hot Prawns 45

Awesome Cherry Tomato Mackerel 45

Salt and Pepper Shrimp 45

Lemon and Pepper Salmon Delight 45

Packets of Lemon and Dill Cod 46

Fish Fillet with Pesto Sauce 46

The Rich Guy Lobster and Butter 46

Lovely Panko Cod 47

Heartfelt Air Fried Scampi 47

Buttered Up Scallops 47

Alaskan Cod Divine 47

Awesome Sock-Eye Salmon 48

Lovely Air Fried Scallops 48

Lemon Garlic Shrimp 48

Fresh Steamed Salmon 49

Chapter 5: Vegan and Vegetarian Recipes 50

Tofu, Broccoli and Carrot 50

Smoked Chickpeas 50

Buffalo Cauliflower 50

Garlic Pepper Potato Chips 51

Crispy Tofu 51

Crazy Fresh Onion Soup 51

Fried Tempeh 52

Garlic Chips 52

Delicious Beet Borscht 52

Cauliflower Stir Fry 53

Feisty Maple Dredged Carrots 53

Onion Rings 53

Elegant Zero Crust Kale and Mushroom Quiche 53

Vegan Cheese Sticks 54

Slow-Cooked Brussels 54

Fried Soy Curls 54

The Creative Mushroom Stroganoff 54

Very Rich and Creamy Asparagus Soup 55

Garlic and Ginger Red Cabbage Platter 55

Cheddar Cauliflower Bowl 55

Potato Wedges 56

The Original Sicilian Cauliflower Roast 56

Slowly Cooked Lemon Artichokes 56

The Authentic Zucchini Pesto Meal 57

Supreme Cauliflower Soup 57

Fried Broccoli 57

Brussels Sprouts 57

A Prosciutto and Thyme Eggs 58

Vegetable Fritters 58

The Veggie Lover's Onion and Tofu Platter 58

Pepper Jack Cauliflower Meal 59

Well Dressed Brussels 59

Summertime Vegetable Platter 59

Chapter 6: Soups and Stews Recipes 60

Chicken & Lemon Soup 60

Cauliflower Soup 60

Beef & Vegetable Soup 60

Beef & Potato Stew 61

Potato Soup 61

Minestrone Soup 62

Tomato Basil Soup 62

Ham & Potato Soup 63

Chapter 7: Snacks, Appetizers & Sides Recipes 64

Honey Mustard Hot Dogs 64

Cheesy Tangy Arancini 64

Chicken Wings 64

Artichoke Bites 65

Zesty Brussels Sprouts with Raisins 65

Eggplant Chips with Honey 65

Asparagus Wrapped in Prosciutto with Garbanzo

Dip. 66

Cheesy Smashed Sweet Potatoes 66

Cheesy Cauliflower Tater Tots 66

Buttery Chicken Meatballs 67

Steak and Minty Cheese 67

Barbecue Chicken Drumsticks 67

Teriyaki Chicken Wings 68

Sweet Pickled Cucumbers 68

Fried Beef Dumplings 68

Crispy Cheesy Straws 69

Herby Fish Skewers 69

Cheesy Cabbage Side Dish 69

Fried Pin Wheels 69

Creamy Tomato Parsley Dip 70

Turkey Scotch Eggs 70

Cheesy Tomato Bruschetta 70

Rosemary Potato Fries 70

Rosemary and Garlic Mushrooms 71

Chicken Meatballs with Ranch Dip 71

Cheesy Brazilian Balls 71

Cheesy Bacon Dip 72

Cheese bombs wrapped in Bacon. 72

Spinach Hummus 72

Egg Brulee 72

Cumin Baby Carrots 73

Wrapped Asparagus in Bacon 73

Mouthwatering Meatballs 73

Green Vegan Dip 73

Chicken and Cheese Bake 74

Chapter 8: Desserts Recipes 75

Ginger Cookies 75

Vanilla Creme Brulee 75

Pecan Muffins 75

Vanilla Muffins 76

Sweet Zucchini Crisp 76

Keto Brownie Batter 76

Mint Cake 77

Chocolate Cakes 77

Pumpkin Pie 77

Cinnamon Bun 78

Chip Cookies 78

Cinnamon Bites 78

Keto Brownie 79

Keto Donuts 79

Pumpkin Muffins 79

Avocado Mousse 79

Lava Cups 80

Mini Cheesecakes 80

Coconut Pie 80

Blackberry Cake 81

Raspberry Dump Cake 81

Vanilla Custard 81

Peanut Butter Cookies 82

Tender Pudding 82

Almond Bites 82

Introduction

The Ninja Foodi—The pressure cooker that crisps. Pressure cooker, air fryer, tender crisper. It comes with a 6.5 quart ceramic-coated pot with enough capacity to cook for your entire family. Whether you want to cook your meals faster or with less oil, Ninja Foodi has you covered. Tender crisp technology allows you to quickly cook ingredients, then the crisping lid gives your meals a crispy, golden finish.

The Ninja Foodi Pressure Cooker is very powerful. We need to understand its functions and store a variety of recipes so that we can maximize its value. So, we need professional books to guide the correct use. The Ninja Foodi Pressure Cooker Cookbook will give you the perfect recipe. We tested the recipe extensively to ensure its quality. At the same time, we have accurate preparation time, cooking time, bill of materials, steps, and nutritional content data for each dish.

The book will provide you with a complete set of The Ninja Foodi Pressure Cooker Cookbook. The recipes include Breakfast, Beef and Pork, Chicken and Poultry, Fish and Seafood, Vegetarian Dishes, Dessert, etc. This book can fully meet your daily cooking needs.
Let the book help you enjoy the most beautiful food in the world.

Chapter 1: Breakfast Recipes

Classical Fried Eggs

Prep time: 5 min, Cooking time: 10 min, Serves: 2

Ingredients
- 4 eggs
- 1 teaspoon butter
- ¼ teaspoon ground black pepper
- ¾ teaspoon salt

Directions
1. Grease the small egg pan with the butter.
2. Beat the eggs in the egg pan and sprinkle with the ground black pepper and salt.
3. Transfer the egg pan in the pot and lower the air fryer lid.
4. Cook the eggs for 10 min at 350 F.
5. Serve the cooked eggs immediately!

Nutrition value/serving: calories 143, fat 10.7, fiber 0.1, carbs 0.9, protein 11.1

Cheese Casserole

Prep time: 5 min, Cooking time: 22 min, Serves: 2

Ingredients
- 1 oz bacon, chopped
- 2 eggs, whisked
- ¼ cup almond milk
- ½ teaspoon dried basil
- 3 oz Cheddar cheese

Directions
1. Mix up together the whisked eggs, almond milk and dried basil.
2. Add bacon and transfer the mixture into the springform pan.
3. Grate cheese and sprinkle it over the egg mixture.
4. Place the casserole into the Foodi and set "Air Crisp" mode 365 F.
5. Cook the casserole for 15 min.
6. Check the casserole and cook it for 5-7 min more.
7. Serve it!

Nutrition value/serving: calories 380, fat 31.5, fiber 0.7, carbs 2.8, protein 22.1

Jalapeno Chicken Wings

Prep time: 15 min, Cooking time: 15 min, Serves: 4

Ingredients
- 12 oz chicken wings
- 2 jalapeno peppers, chopped
- 1 teaspoon minced garlic
- 1 tablespoon coconut oil
- ¼ cup of water
- 1 tablespoon butter
- ½ teaspoon salt

Directions
1. Blend together the jalapeno peppers and minced garlic until smooth.
2. Then combine together the pepper mixture, salt, and coconut oil.
3. Brush every chicken wing with the pepper mixture and let for 10 min to marinate.
4. Place the marinated chicken wings in the pot. Add butter and water.
5. Close the lid and seal it.
6. Cook the chicken wings for 10 min on High 9Pressure mode).
7. Then make a quick pressure release.
8. Lower the air fryer lid and cook the chicken wings for 5 min more at 400 F.
9. Serve!

Nutrition value/serving: calories 220, fat 12.7, fiber 0.3, carbs 0.8, protein 24.8

Asparagus Frittata

Prep time: 10 min, Cooking time: 21 min, Serves: 2

Ingredients
- 2 oz asparagus, chopped
- 3 eggs, whisked
- 2 tablespoons almond milk
- 1 teaspoon almond flour
- ½ teaspoon salt
- ¼ teaspoon cayenne pepper
- ½ oz Parmesan, grated
- 1 teaspoon coconut oil

Directions
1. Preheat the pot on "Sauté/Stear mode.
2. Add coconut oil and chopped asparagus.

3. Sauté the vegetable for 3 min.
4. Meanwhile, mix up together the almond milk, whisked, eggs, almond flour, cayenne pepper, and grated cheese.
5. Pour the egg mixture into the pot.
6. Close the lid and seal it.
7. Cook the frittata on High (Pressure mode) for 15 min.
8. After this, make a quick pressure release.
9. Lower the air fryer lid and cook the meal at 400 F for 6 min more.
10. When the surface of the frittata is crusty enough – finish cooking and serve it!

Nutrition value/serving: calories 165, fat 12.3, fiber 1.1, carbs 3.1, protein 11.8

Curry Shredded Chicken

Prep time: 10 min, Cooking time: 35 min, Serves: 2

Ingredients
- 1-pound chicken breast, skinless, boneless
- 1 teaspoon curry paste
- 2 tablespoons butter
- 1 teaspoon cayenne pepper
- ½ cup of water

Directions
1. Rub the chicken breast with the curry paste and place in the pot.
2. Sprinkle the poultry with cayenne pepper and add butter.
3. Pour water in the pot and close the lid. Seal the lid.
4. Set Pressure mode and cook on High for 30 min.
5. Then make natural pressure release for 10 min.
6. Open the lid and shred the chicken inside the pot with the help of the fork.
7. Then close the lid and sauté the chicken for 5 min more.
8. Serve it!

Nutrition value/serving: calories 380, fat 18.8, fiber 0.2, carbs 1.2, protein 48.4

Parmesan Chicken Wings

Prep time: 10 min, Cooking time: 17 min, Serves: 2

Ingredients
- 4 chicken wings
- ½ cup chicken stock
- ½ teaspoon salt
- 1 tablespoon butter, softened
- 1oz Parmesan, grated
- 1 teaspoon garlic powder
- 1 teaspoon minced garlic
- 1 teaspoon dried dill

Directions
1. Rub the chicken wings with the salt and place in the Ninja Foodi pot.
2. Add chicken stock and close the lid.
3. Seal the lid and cook chicken wings at Pressure Cook mode (High pressure) for 9 min.
4. Meanwhile, mix up together the butter, grated cheese, minced garlic, garlic powder, and dried dill. Whisk the mixture until homogenous.
5. When the chicken wings are cooked – make a quick pressure release. Open the lid and transfer chicken wings on the plate.
6. Remove the liquid from the pot and insert rack.
7. Brush the chicken wings with the butter mixture generously and transfer on the rack.
8. Lower the air fryer lid and press the "Broil" mode.
9. Cook the wings for 8 min.
10. Enjoy!

Nutrition value/serving: calories 192, fat 12.4, fiber 0.2, carbs 2.4, protein 18

Green Beans Omelet

Prep time: 7 min, Cooking time: 14 min, Serves: 2

Ingredients
- 3 eggs, whisked
- 1 tablespoon cream cheese
- 1 oz green beans
- 1 teaspoon butter
- ¼ teaspoon salt
- ¼ teaspoon chili flakes

Directions
1. Preheat Ninja Foodi on Sauté/Stear mode.
2. Toss butter inside.
3. Add green beans and sauté them for 4 min.
4. Meanwhile, whisk together the eggs and cream cheese.
5. Add salt and chili flakes. Stir the liquid.

6. Pour the liquid in the pot and stir gently with the help of a spatula.
7. Lower the air fryer lid and cook an omelet for 10 min at 360 F.
8. Serve it!
Nutrition value/serving: calories 133, fat 10.2, fiber 0.5, carbs 1.7, protein 9

Low Carb Morning Casserole

Prep time: 5 min, Cooking time: 10 min, Serves: 3
Ingredients
- 3 oz cauliflower hash brown, cooked
- 3 eggs, whisked
- ¾ cup almond milk
- 2 oz chorizo, chopped
- 1 oz mozzarella, sliced
- 1/3 teaspoon chili flakes
- ½ teaspoon butter

Directions
1. Melt the butter and whisk it together with the chili flakes, chorizo, almond milk, and eggs.
2. Add hash brown and stir gently.
3. Place the egg mixture in the cake pan and place in the Ninja Foodi.
4. Cook on Air Crisp 365 F for 8 min.
5. Then add sliced mozzarella on the top and cook for 2 min more, or until you get the desired doneness.
6. Enjoy!
Nutrition value/serving: calories 326, fat 28.2, fiber 1.9, carbs 5.8, protein 14.7

Eggs in Bacon Cups

Prep time: 10 min, Cooking time: 15 min, Serves: 4
Ingredients
- 4 eggs
- 1 tablespoon butter
- 1 teaspoon dried parsley
- ¼ teaspoon cayenne pepper
- ¼ teaspoons paprika
- 4 bacon strips
- 1 oz Parmesan, grated

Directions
1. Grease the small ramekins with butter.
2. Then secure the bacon strips on the edges of every ramekin.
3. Beat the egg in the center of every ramekin.
4. Sprinkle the eggs with paprika, dried parsley, cayenne pepper, and cheese.
5. Place the ramekins in the pot and lower the air fryer lid.
6. Cook the egg at 365 F for 15 min.
7. Chill the meal little and serve!
Nutrition value/serving: calories 212, fat 17.8, fiber 0.1, carbs 0.7, protein 11.9

Asparagus and Bacon Plate

Prep time: 6 min, Cooking time: 9 min, Serves: 2
Ingredients
- 2 oz bacon, chopped
- 4 oz asparagus, chopped
- ½ teaspoon salt
- ½ teaspoon ground black pepper
- 1 tablespoon butter
- 1 cup water, for cooking

Directions
1. Place the bacon on the air fryer rack and sprinkle with the ground black pepper.
2. Lower the air fryer lid and cook the bacon at 400 F for 8 min.
3. Flip the bacon into another side after 4 min of cooking.
4. Then transfer the cooked bacon on the plate.
5. Pour water in the pot and insert steamer rack.
6. Place the asparagus and close the lid.
7. Cook the asparagus on High for 5 min. Then make quick pressure release.
8. Transfer the cooked asparagus over the bacon.
9. Add butter and salt.
10. Serve it!
Nutrition value/serving: calories 217, fat 17.7, fiber 1.3, carbs 3, protein 11.9

Chili Chicken Bites

Prep time: 7 min, Cooking time: 25 min, Serves: 3
Ingredients
- 12 oz chicken fillet
- 1 teaspoon chili flakes
- ½ teaspoon chili pepper
- ½ teaspoon red hot pepper
- ¼ teaspoon ground cumin
- ½ teaspoon salt

- 1 tablespoon butter
- ¾ cup heavy cream

Directions
1. Cut the chicken fillet into the cubes.
2. Mix up together all the spices.
3. Combine together the chicken cubes and spices.
4. Then toss the butter in Ninja Foodi pot and melt it on Sauté/Stear mode.
5. Place the chicken cubes in the pot and Sauté them for 5 min. Stir time to time.
6. After this, add cream and stir well.
7. Lower the air fryer lid and cook the chicken bites at 360 F for 20 min.
8. When the time is over – serve the chicken immediately!

Nutrition value/serving: calories 354, fat 23.4, fiber 0.1, carbs 1.1, protein 33.5

Feta Frittata

Prep time: 10 min, Cooking time: 15 min, Serves: 3

Ingredients
- 4 oz fresh spinach, chopped
- 3 eggs, beaten
- 1 oz Feta, crumbled
- ¼ teaspoon white pepper
- ¼ teaspoon salt

Directions
1. Whisk the eggs well.
2. Stir the spinach in the whisked eggs and add white pepper and salt.
3. After this, add Feta cheese and mix up the egg mixture with the help of the spoon gently
4. Transfer the liquid in the springform pan.
5. Insert the air fryer rack in Ninja Foodi and place the frittata.
6. Lower the air fryer lid and cook frittata at 360 F.
7. Cook for 15 min or until the meal is set. Serve it!

Nutrition value/serving: calories 97, fat 6.5, fiber 0.9, carbs 2.2, protein 8

Fish with Sesame

Prep time: 8 min, Cooking time: 8 min, Serves: 4

Ingredients
- 1.5-pound salmon fillet
- 1 tablespoon apple cider vinegar
- 1 teaspoon sesame seeds
- ¼ teaspoon dried rosemary
- ½ teaspoon salt
- 1 teaspoon butter, melted

Directions
1. Sprinkle the salmon fillet with the apple cider vinegar.
2. After this, mix up together the sesame seeds, dried rosemary, salt, and butter.
3. Brush the salmon with the butter sauce generously.
4. Place the salmon on the rack and lower the air fryer lid.
5. Set the air fryer mode and cook fish at 360 F for 8 min.
6. Serve it!

Nutrition value/serving: calories 239, fat 11.8, fiber 0.1, carbs 0.3, protein 33.1

Hard Boiled Eggs with Bacon Filling

Prep time: 10 min, Cooking time: 15 min, Serves: 2

Ingredients
- 4 eggs
- 1 teaspoon cream cheese
- 1 oz bacon, chopped, cooked
- 1/2 teaspoon minced garlic

Directions
1. Place the eggs in the air fryer basket and lower the air fryer lid.
2. Cook the eggs at 250 F for 15 min.
3. Meanwhile, mix up together the cooked bacon, minced garlic, and cream cheese.
4. When the eggs are cooked – chill them in ice water and peel.
5. Cut the eggs into the halves and transfer the egg yolks in the cream cheese mixture.
6. Stir it carefully until homogenous.
7. Fill the egg whites with the filling and serve!

Nutrition value/serving: calories 205, fat 15.3, fiber 0, carbs 1.2, protein 16.5

Western Omelet

Prep time: 5 min, Cooking time: 34 min, Serves: 2

Ingredients
- 3 eggs, whisked
- 5 tablespoon almond milk
- 3 oz chorizo, chopped
- 1 green pepper, chopped
- ¼ teaspoon salt
- ¾ teaspoon chili flakes
- 1 oz Feta cheese, crumbled

Directions
1. Mix up together all the ingredients and stir gently.
2. Pour the mixture into the omelet pan.
3. Preheat Ninja Foodi at "Roast/Bake" mode at 320 F for 4 min.
4. Then transfer the pan with an omelet in Ninja Foodi and cook at the same mode for 30 min.
5. Serve the cooked meal hot!

Nutrition value/serving: calories 424, fat 34.9, fiber 1.9, carbs 6.8, protein 21.9

Keto Cheddar Bites

Prep time: 6 min, Cooking time: 12 min, Serves: 4

Ingredients
- 4 eggs
- ¼ cup heavy cream
- 3 oz Cheddar cheese, shredded
- 3 oz shrimps, peeled, cooked
- ½ teaspoon salt
- ½ cup of water

Directions
1. Beat the eggs in the bowl and whisk well.
2. Add heavy cream, salt, and cheese. Stir it.
3. Chop the shrimps roughly and add in egg mixture.
4. Pour the egg mixture into the muffin molds.
5. Add water in the pot.
6. Place the muffins molds on the rack.
7. Cover the molds with the foil well.
8. Close the lid and seal it.
9. Cook the bites on High for 12 min. (Natural pressure release)
10. Discard the foil from bites and transfer them on the serving plates. Taste it!

Nutrition value/serving: calories 200, fat 14.6, fiber 0, carbs 1.1, protein 15.8

Keto Juicy Bacon Strips

Prep time: 5 min, Cooking time: 7 min, Serves: 2

Ingredients
- 10 bacon strips
- ¼ teaspoon dried basil
- ¼ teaspoon chili flakes
- 1/3 teaspoon salt

Directions
1. Rub the bacon strips with the dried basil, chili flakes, and salt.
2. Place the bacon on the rack and lower the air fryer lid.
3. Cook the bacon for 5 min at 400 F.
4. Check if the bacon is cooked and cook for 3 min more or until you get the desired doneness.

Nutrition value/serving: calories 500, fat 45, fiber 0, carbs 0, protein 20

Chorizo Fritatta

Prep time: 10 min, Cooking time: 20 min, Serves: 6

Ingredients
- 5 eggs, whisked
- 1 oz fresh parsley, chopped
- 3 oz chorizo, chopped
- 1 teaspoon salt
- ¼ green pepper, chopped
- 1 teaspoon butter
- ¼ cup heavy cream
- 1 oz broccoli, chopped
- 1 oz Cheddar cheese, grated
- 1 teaspoon cream cheese
- 1 teaspoon paprika
- 1 cup of water (for cooking on High pressure)

Directions
1. Grease the springform pan with the butter.
2. Then place the layer of green pepper and broccoli.
3. After this, whisk together eggs, parsley, salt, heavy cream, cream cheese, and paprika.
4. Add chorizo and cheese. Stir gently and transfer the mixture in the pan. Flatten it gently.
5. Pour water in the pan and place the springform cake on the rack.

6. Close the lid and seal it.
7. Cook the meal on High (Pressure mode) for 20 min. Then use the quick pressure release method for 5 min.
8. Serve it!

Nutrition value/serving: calories 166, fat 13.4, fiber 0.5, carbs 1.8, protein 9.7

Breakfast Pork Chops

Prep time: 10 min, Cooking time: 30 min, Serves: 2

Ingredients
- 2 pork chops
- 1 teaspoon butter
- ½ teaspoon dried cilantro
- 1 oz Mozzarella, sliced
- ½ teaspoon cayenne pepper
- ¾ cup of water

Directions
1. Sprinkle the pork chops with the dried cilantro and cayenne pepper.
2. Toss the butter in Foodi and melt it on Sauté/Stear mode.
3. Add pork chops and cook them for 2 min from each side.
4. Add water and close the lid.
5. Cook the meat on "Sauté/Stear" mode for 25 min.
6. When the pork chops are cooked – open the lid and cover the meat with the sliced cheese.
7. Lower the air fryer lid and cook the meat for 3 min more at 400 F.
8. Enjoy!

Nutrition value/serving: calories 314, fat 24.4, fiber 0.1, carbs 0.8, protein 22.1

Quiche Lorraine

Prep time: 10 min, Cooking time: 15 min, Serves: 4

Ingredients
- 4 eggs, whisked
- ½ teaspoon salt
- ½ teaspoon cayenne pepper
- ¼ cup heavy cream
- 2 oz bacon, chopped
- 1 tablespoon butter
- 3oz Parmesan, grated
- ½ teaspoon dried basil

Directions
1. Preheat Ninja Foodi at "Sauté/Stear" mode for 5 min.
2. Then add butter and melt it.
3. Add bacon and sauté it for 4 min.
4. Meanwhile, whisk together the eggs, salt, cayenne pepper, dried basil, and heavy cream.
5. When the bacon is cooked – add the egg mixture and lower the air fryer lid.
6. Cook the meal for 10 min at 365 F.
7. Then top the egg mixture with the grated cheese and cook for 5 min more.
8. Serve it!

Nutrition value/serving: calories 260, fat 20.5, fiber 0.1, carbs 1.6, protein 17.8

Chicken Sandwiches

Prep time: 10 min, Cooking time: 15 min, Serves: 4

Ingredients
- 1-pound chicken thighs, boneless, skinless
- 1 cup lettuce
- 1 teaspoon apple cider vinegar
- ½ teaspoon chili flakes
- 1 teaspoon red hot pepper
- ½ teaspoon turmeric
- 1 teaspoon white pepper
- ½ cup of water
- 1 tablespoon low-sodium soy sauce
- 1 tablespoon butter
- 1 oz Cheddar cheese, shredded

Directions
1. Preheat Ninja Foodi at Sauté/Stear mode for 5 min.
2. Toss the butter inside the pot.
3. Then rub the chicken thighs with the chili flakes, red hot pepper, turmeric, white pepper, and sprinkle with the soy sauce and apple cider vinegar.
4. Place the chicken in the pot and cook it for 5 min.
5. After this, close the lid and seal it.
6. Cook the chicken on High pressure for 5 min – quick pressure release).
7. After this, shred the chicken and remove ½ part of all the liquid from the form.
8. Lower the air fryer lid and cook the chicken at 400 F for 5 min more.

9. Transfer the cooked chicken on the lettuce leaves and sprinkle with cheese.
10. Taste it!

Nutrition value/serving: calories 276, fat 13.7, fiber 0.3, carbs 1.4, protein 35

Breakfast Muffins

Prep time: 10 min, Cooking time: 15 min, Serves: 2

Ingredients
- 1 tablespoon cream cheese
- 1 teaspoon butter
- 1 egg, beaten
- 1 tablespoon almond flour
- 2 oz Cheddar cheese, grated
- ¼ teaspoon ground black pepper
- ½ teaspoon salt
- ½ teaspoon paprika
- ½ cup water (for cooking on High)

Directions
1. Mix up together the cream cheese, butter, egg, almond flour, cheese, ground black pepper, salt, and paprika.
2. Whisk the mixture until smooth.
3. After this, pour ½ cup of water in the pot. Insert the rack.
4. Transfer the batter in the prepared muffins molds and place on the rack.
5. Cover the muffins with the foil and close the lid.
6. Make sure you seal the lid and cook on PRESSURE mode (High) for 15 min.
7. Then make the quick pressure release for 5 min.
8. Chill the muffins little and serve!

Nutrition value/serving: calories 203, fat 17, fiber 0.7, carbs 1.9, protein 11.1

Bacon Jalapeno

Prep time: 6 min, Cooking time: 3 min, Serves: 3

Ingredients
- 6 jalapeno peppers
- 1 teaspoon minced garlic
- 6 tablespoon cream cheese
- 6 bacon strips, chopped, cooked
- ½ teaspoon salt
- 1 oz ground beef, cooked
- ¼ teaspoon ground cumin

Directions
1. Trim the ends of the peppers and remove all the seeds from inside.
2. Mix up together the minced garlic, cream cheese, salt, and ground cumin. Add the ground beef and stir well. Add bacon.
3. Fill the peppers with the mixture and transfer on the rack.
4. Lower the air fryer lid and cook the jalapenos for min at 365 F.
5. Serve the meal immediately!

Nutrition value/serving: calories 301, fat 26, fiber 1.2, carbs 3, protein 12.9

Eggs in Mushroom Hats

Prep time: 10 min, Cooking time: 9 min, Serves: 1

Ingredients
- 4 oz mushroom hats
- 4 quail eggs
- ¼ teaspoon salt
- ½ teaspoon ground black pepper
- 1 teaspoon butter, melted

Directions
1. Spread the mushroom hats with the butter inside.
2. Then beat the eggs into the mushroom hats and sprinkle with the ground black pepper and salt.
3. Transfer the mushroom hats on the rack and lower the air fryer lid.
4. Cook the meal at 365 F for 7 min.
5. Then check the mushrooms and cook them for 2 min more.
6. Serve it!

Nutrition value/serving: calories 118, fat 8.2, fiber 1., carbs 4.6, protein 8.4

Butter Chicken Bites

Prep time: 10 min, Cooking time: 11 min, Serves: 3

Ingredients
- 10 oz chicken thighs, boneless, skinless
- 1 teaspoon turmeric
- 1 teaspoon chili flakes
- ½ teaspoon salt
- ¼ teaspoon ground nutmeg
- ¾ teaspoon ground ginger
- ½ cup heavy cream

- 2 tablespoon butter
- 1 teaspoon kosher salt

Directions
1. Preheat Ninja Foodi pot at Sauté /Stear mode for 5 min.
2. Toss the butter in the pot and melt it.
3. Add turmeric, chili flakes, salt, and ground nutmeg. Then, add ground ginger and salt.
4. Bring to boil the mixture.
5. Meanwhile, chop the chicken thighs roughly.
6. Transfer the chicken thighs in the pot and cooks for 5 min at Sauté mode.
7. After this, add heavy cream and close the lid. Seal the lid.
8. Select Pressure mode and set High pressure
9. Cook it for 6 min. Then make a quick pressure release.
10. Chill the cooked chicken bites little and serve!

Nutrition value/serving: calories 322, fat 22.3, fiber 0.3, carbs 1.5, protein 28

Chapter 2: Beef, Lamb and Pork Recipes

Delicious Braised Pork Neck Bones

Prep + Cooking Time: 40 min, Serves: 6

Ingredients
- 3 lbs. Pork Neck Bones
- 4 tbsp. Olive Oil
- 1 White Onion, sliced
- 1/2 cup Red Wine
- 2 cloves Garlic, smashed
- 1 tbsp. Tomato Paste
- 1 tsp. dried Thyme
- 1 cup Beef Broth
- Salt and Black Pepper to taste

Directions

1. Open the lid and select Sear/Sauté mode. Warm the olive oil
2. Meanwhile season the pork neck bones with salt and pepper. After, place them in the oil to brown on all sides. Work in batches.
3. Each batch should cook in about 5 min. Then, remove them onto a plate.
4. Add the onion and season with salt to taste. Stir with a spoon and cook the onions until soft, for a few min. Then, add garlic, thyme, pepper, and tomato paste. Cook them for 2 min, constant stirring to prevent the tomato paste from burning
5. Next, pour the red wine into the pot to deglaze the bottom. Add the pork neck bones back to the pot and pour the beef broth over it
6. Close the lid, secure the pressure valve, and select Pressure mode on High pressure for 10 min. Press Start/Stop to start cooking.
7. Once the timer has ended, let the pot sit for 10 min before doing a quick pressure release. Close the crisping lid and cook on Broil mode for 5 min, until nice and tender.
8. Dish the pork neck into a serving bowl and serve with the red wine sauce spooned over and a right amount of broccoli mash

Pot Roast

Prep + Cooking Time: 1 hour 50 min, Serves: 4 to 6

Ingredients
- 1 3- to 3½ lb. boneless beef chuck roast
- 1 ½ lb. small white or yellow potatoes
- 1/2-ounce dried mushrooms, preferably porcini
- 1 tbsp. olive oil
- 1 large yellow onion, chopped.
- 2 tsp. minced garlic
- 1 ½ cups beef broth
- 3 tbsp. tomato paste
- 1 4-inch rosemary sprig
- 1 tsp. salt
- 1/2 tsp. ground black pepper

Directions

1. Heat the oil in the Ninja Foodi Multi-cooker. Turn on the Multi-cooker to the Sauté setting then wait for it to boil.
2. Season the roast with the salt and pepper; brown it on both sides, turning once, about 10 min. Transfer the meat to a large bowl.
3. Add the onion; cook, often stirring, until translucent, about 4 min. Add the garlic; cook, stirring constantly, until aromatic, about 30 seconds. Pour 1 ¼ cup broth in the Ninja Foodi Multi-cooker.
4. Add the tomato paste and stir well until dissolved. Tuck the rosemary into the sauce and crumble in the mushrooms. Nestle the meat into the sauce, adding any juices in the bowl
5. High pressure for 60 min. Close the lid and the pressure valve and then cook for 60 min
6. To get 60 min' cook time, press *Pressure* button and use the Time Adjustment button to adjust the cook time to 60 min
7. Pressure Release. Use the quick release method.
8. Unlock and open the cooker; sprinkle the potatoes around the meat
9. High pressure for 30 min. Close the lid and the pressure valve again and cook for 30 min.
10. To get 30 min' cook time, press *Pressure* button
11. Pressure Release. Use the natural release method 20 to 30 min

12. Finish the dish. Close crisping lid. Select "BROIL" and set time to 8 min. Check after 5 min, cooking for an additional 3 min if dish needs more browning
13. Transfer the roast to a cutting board; set aside for 5 min. Discard the rosemary sprig.
14. Slice the meat into 2-inch irregular chunks and serve these in bowls with the vegetables, mushrooms and broth. Serve

Beef Chili & Cornbread Casserole

Prep + Cooking Time: 60 min, Serves: 8
Ingredients
- 2 lb. uncooked ground beef
- 3 cans 14-ounces each kidney beans, rinsed, drained
- 1 can 28-ounces crushed tomatoes
- 1 cup beef stock
- 1 large white onion, peeled, diced
- 1 green bell pepper, diced
- 1 jalapeño pepper, diced, seeds removed
- 4 cloves garlic, peeled, minced
- 2 tbsp. kosher salt
- 1 tbsp. ground black pepper
- 2 tbsp. ground cumin
- 1 tbsp. onion powder
- 1 tbsp. garlic powder
- 2 cups Cheddar Corn Bread batter, uncooked
- 1 cup shredded Mexican cheese blend
- Sour cream, for serving

Directions
1. Place beef, beans, tomatoes, and stock into the pot, breaking apart meat. Assemble pressure lid, making sure the PRESSURE RELEASE valve is in the SEAL position. Select PRESSURE and set to HIGH. Set time to 15 min. Select START/STOP to begin.
2. When pressure cooking is complete, quick release the pressure by moving the PRESSURE RELEASE valve to the VENT position. Carefully remove lid when unit has finished releasing pressure
3. Select SEAR/SAUTÉ. Set temperature to MD, Select START/STOP. Add onion, green bell pepper, jalapeño pepper, garlic, and spices; stir to incorporate. Bring to a simmer and cook for 5 min, stirring occasionally.
4. Dollop corn bread batter evenly over the top of the chili. Close crisping lid. Select BAKE/ROAST, set temperature to 360°F, and set time to 26 min. Select START/STOP to begin.
5. After 15 min, open lid and insert a wooden toothpick into the center of the corn bread. If corn bread is not done, close lid to resume cooking for another 8 min
6. When corn bread is done, sprinkle it with cheese and close lid to resume cooking for 3 min, or until cheese is melted. When cooking is complete, top with sour cream and serve

Macaroni and Cheese

Prep + Cooking Time: 20 min, Serves: 4
Ingredients
- 1 lb. elbow macaroni
- 1 cup breadcrumbs
- ½ cup bacon; chopped.
- 3 cups chicken stock
- 1 cup water
- 3 cups mozzarella, shredded
- ½ stick of butter, melted
- Salt and black pepper to the taste

Directions
1. Put the stock, water and the pasta in the Foodi machine, put the pressure lid on and cook on Low for 10 min. Release the pressure naturally for 10 min.
2. Add the cheese, butter, breadcrumbs, bacon, salt and pepper, toss, leave aside for 10 more min, divide between plates and serve

Easy Sausage and Peppers

Prep + Cooking Time: 25 min, Serves: 5 to 6
Ingredients
- 2 ½ lb. sweet Italian sausages in their casings
- 1 medium red onion, halved and thinly sliced
- 2 medium garlic cloves, slivered
- 1 cup red sweet vermouth
- 4 large red bell peppers, stemmed, seeded and cut into strips
- 2 tbsp. olive oil
- 2 tbsp. balsamic vinegar
- 1/4 tsp. grated nutmeg

Directions

1. Heat the oil in a Ninja Foodi Multi-cooker, turned to the sauté function. Prick the sausages with a fork, add them to the pot and brown on all sides, about 6 min. Transfer to a large bowl.
2. Add the peppers and onion; cook, stirring almost constantly, just until the pepper strips glisten, about 2 min
3. Add the garlic, cook a few seconds and then stir in the vermouth, vinegar and nutmeg. Nestle the sausages into the mixture.
4. High pressure for 10 min. Lock the lid on the Ninja Foodi Multi-cooker and Cook for 10 min.
5. To get 10 min' cook time, press the *Pressure* button and adjust the time
6. Pressure Release. Use the quick release method to bring the pot's pressure back to normal
7. Remove the lid from the Ninja Foodi Multi-cooker. Close crisping lid. Select *Air Crisp*, set temperature to 390°F and set time to 10 min.
8. Check after 8 min, cooking for an additional 2 min if dish needs more browning. Stir well before serving.

Chinese Style Beef

Prep + Cooking Time: 25 min, Serves: 2
Ingredients
- 1 lb. beef meat, cut into strips
- 1 yellow onion; chopped.
- 8 oz. shiitake mushrooms, sliced
- 2 tbsp. dark soy sauce
- 1 tsp. olive oil
- Salt and black pepper to the taste

Directions
1. Set the Foodi on Sauté mode, add the oil and heat it up. Add the onion, stir and sauté for 3-4 min. Add the mushrooms, soy sauce and the beef, stir and cook for 2-3 min more
2. Add salt and pepper, put the pressure lid on and cook on High for 8 min. Release the pressure naturally for 10 min, divide everything into bowls and serve

Easy Short Ribs and Root Vegetables

Prep + Cooking Time: 1 hour 15 min, Serves: 6
Ingredients

- 6 uncooked bone-in beef short ribs about 3 lb., trimmed of excess fat and silver skin
- 2 tsp. kosher salt, divided.
- 3 carrots, peeled, cut in 1-inch pieces
- 3 parsnips, peeled, cut in 1-inch pieces
- 2 tsp. black pepper, divided.
- 3 cloves garlic, peeled, minced
- 1 onion, peeled, chopped.
- 1/4 cup Marsala wine
- 1/4 cup beef broth
- 2 tbsp. brown sugar
- 2 tbsp. fresh thyme, minced, divided.
- 2 tbsp. olive oil, divided.
- 1 cup pearl onions
- 1/4 cup fresh parsley, minced

Directions
1. Season short ribs on all sides with 1 tsp. salt and 1 tsp. pepper. Select SEAR/SAUTÉ and set to HIGH. Select START/STOP to begin. Heat 1 tbsp. oil in the pot for 3 min.
2. After 3 min, add short ribs to pot and cook until browned on all sides, about 10 min
3. Add onion, wine, broth, brown sugar, garlic, 1 tbsp. thyme, 1/2 tsp. salt, and 1/2 tsp. pepper to pot. Assemble pressure lid, making sure the PRESSURE RELEASE valve is in the SEAL position. Select PRESSURE and set to HIGH. Set time to 40 min. Select START/STOP to begin
4. Toss carrots, parsnips, and pearl onions with remaining oil, thyme, salt, and pepper
5. When pressure cooking is complete, quick release the pressure by moving the PRESSURE RELEASE valve to the VENT position. Carefully remove lid when unit has finished releasing pressure.
6. Place the reversible rack inside pot over ribs, making sure rack is in the higher position. Place vegetable mixture on rack. Close crisping lid. Select BAKE/ROAST, set temperature to 350°F, and set time to 15 min. Select START/STOP to begin
7. Once vegetables are tender and roasted, transfer them and the ribs to a serving tray and tent loosely with aluminum foil to keep warm
8. Select SEAR/SAUTÉ and set to HIGH. Bring liquid in pot to simmer for 5 min. Transfer to bowl and let sit for 2 min, then spoon off top layer of fat.

Stir in parsley. When cooking is complete, serve sauce with vegetables and ribs.

Beef and Spinach

Prep + Cooking Time: 30 min, Serves: 4
Ingredients
- 1 lb. beef meat, ground
- 5 oz. baby spinach
- 1 yellow onion; chopped.
- 3 leeks, roughly chopped
- 2 tbsp. tomato puree
- 1 tbsp. olive oil
- Salt and black pepper to the taste

Directions
1. Set the Foodi on Sauté mode, add the oil and heat it up. Add the onion, stir and cook for 5 min. Add the leeks, stir and cook for 2 min more
2. Add the beef, salt, pepper, tomato puree and the spinach, toss, put the pressure lid on and cook on High for 10 min. Release the pressure naturally for 10 min, divide everything into bowls and serve

Beef Soup

Prep + Cooking Time: 40 min, Serves: 6
Ingredients
- 2 and ½ lbs. beef stew meat; cubed.
- 15 oz. canned tomatoes; chopped.
- 1 yellow onion; chopped.
- 4 carrots; chopped.
- 4 celery stalks; chopped.
- 6 cups beef stock
- 1 cup pearl barley
- 1 tsp. oregano, dried
- 1 tbsp. olive oil
- 2 tbsp. tomato paste
- A pinch of salt and black pepper

Directions
1. Set the Foodi on sauté mode, add the oil, heat it up, add the beef, brown it for 5 min and transfer to a plate. Add the onion, celery, carrots, oregano, salt and pepper to the machine, stir and cook for another 5 min
2. Add the tomatoes, tomato paste, the barley, the stock and the beef, put the pressure lid on and cook on High for 25 min. Release the pressure naturally for 10 min, divide the soup into bowls and serve

Tex-Mex Meatloaf Recipe

Prep + Cooking Time: 45 min, Serves: 8
Ingredients
- 1 lb. uncooked ground beef
- 1 tbsp. garlic powder
- 2 tsp. ground cumin
- 2 tsp. chili powder
- 1 tsp. cayenne pepper
- 1 egg
- 1 bell pepper, diced
- 2 tsp. kosher salt
- 1/4 cup fresh cilantro leaves
- 1/4 barbecue sauce, divided.
- 1/2 jalapeño pepper, seeds removed, minced
- 1 small onion, peeled, diced
- 3 corn tortillas, roughly chopped.
- 1 cup water
- 1 cup corn chips, crushed

Directions
1. Stir together beef, egg, bell pepper, jalapeño pepper, onion, tortillas, spices, cilantro, and tbsp. barbecue sauce in a large mixing bowl.
2. Place meat mixture in the 8 ½-inch loaf pan and cover tightly with aluminum foil
3. Pour water into pot. Place the loaf pan on the reversible rack, making sure rack is in the lower position. Place rack with pan in pot. Assemble the pressure lid, making sure the PRESSURE RELEASE valve is in the SEAL position
4. Select PRESSURE and set to HIGH. Set time to 15 min. Select START/STOP to begin
5. When pressure cooking is complete, quick release the pressure by moving the PRESSURE RELEASE valve to the VENT position. Carefully remove lid when unit has finished releasing pressure
6. Carefully remove foil from loaf pan and close crisping lid. Select BAKE/ROAST, set temperature to 360°F, and set time to 15 min. Select START/STOP to begin.
7. While the meatloaf is cooking, stir together the crushed corn chips and 2 tbsp. barbecue sauce in a bowl.
8. After 7 min, open lid and top meatloaf with the corn chip mixture. Close lid to resume cooking.

When cooking is complete, remove meatloaf from pot and allow to cool for 10 min before serving

Delicious Beef Recipe

Prep + Cooking Time: 30 min, Serves: 4

Ingredients
- 1 ½ lbs. flank steak, sliced
- 4 cups broccoli florets
- 4 scallions; chopped.
- ½ cup beef stock
- ½ cup water
- ½ cup soy sauce
- 2 tbsp. brown sugar
- 2 tbsp. cornstarch
- 1 tbsp. ginger; grated.
- 3 tbsp. sherry
- A pinch of salt and black pepper

Directions

1. In a bowl mix the stock with the soy sauce, sherry, sugar, ginger, salt and pepper and whisk well. Add the steaks, toss and leave aside for 10 min
2. Put the water in the Foodi, place the basket inside and put the broccoli in the basket. Put the pressure lid on, set the Foodi to Steam mode, cook the broccoli for 5 min and transfer it to a bowl
3. Clean the pot, add the broccoli, the beef, cornstarch and scallions, toss, put the pressure lid on and cook on High for 10 min.
4. Release the pressure naturally for 10 min, divide everything between plates and serve

Sausage and Chard Pasta Sauce

Prep + Cooking Time: 18 min, Serves: 5 to 6

Ingredients
- 1-lb. mild Italian pork sausage meat, any casings removed
- 3 small hot chiles, such as cherry peppers or Anaheim chiles, stemmed, seeded and chopped.
- 1 medium red onion, chopped.
- 1/2 cup dry red wine, such as Syrah
- 1/2 cup canned tomato paste
- 1/4 cup chicken broth
- 4 cups stemmed and chopped Swiss chard
- 2 tbsp. olive oil
- 1 tbsp. minced garlic
- 1 tbsp. dried basil
- 2 tsp. dried oregano

Directions

1. Heat the oil in a Ninja Foodi Multi-cooker, turned to the sauté function.
2. Add the onion and cook, often stirring, until softened, about 4 min. Add the chiles and garlic; cook until aromatic, stirring all the while, about 1 minute.
3. Crumble in the sausage meat, breaking up any clumps with a wooden spoon.
4. Stir until it loses its raw color. Stir in the wine, tomato paste, broth, basil and oregano until the tomato paste dissolves. Add the chard and stir well
5. High pressure for 6 min. Lock the lid onto the cooker, set the machine's timer to cook at high pressure for 6 min
6. To get 6 min' cook time, press the *Pressure* button and use the Time Adjustment button to adjust the cook time to 6 min.
7. Pressure Release. Use the quick release method to drop the pressure back to normal.
8. Finish the dish. Remove the lid from the Ninja Foodi Multi-cooker. Close crisping lid. Select "BROIL" and set time to 5 min
9. Check after 4 min, cooking for an additional 4 min if dish needs more browning. Stir well before serving

Pork Shoulder Chops with Carrots

Prep + Cooking Time: 70 min, Serves: 4 to 6

Ingredients
- 3 lb. bone in pork shoulder chops, each 1/2 to 3/4 inch thick
- 6 medium carrots
- 1/3 cup maple syrup
- 1/3 cup chicken broth
- 3 medium garlic cloves
- 1 tbsp. bacon fat
- 1/3 cup soy sauce
- 1/2 tsp. ground black pepper

Directions

1. Melt the bacon fat in a Ninja Foodi Multi-cooker, turned to the browning function. Add about half the chops and brown well, turning once, about 5 min.

Transfer these to a large bowl and brown the remaining chops

2. Stir the carrots and garlic into the pot; cook for 1 minute, constantly stirring. Pour in the soy sauce, maple syrup and broth, stirring to dissolve the maple syrup and to get up any browned bits on the bottom of the pot. Stir in the pepper. Return the shoulder chops and their juices to the pot. Stir to coat them in the sauce

3. High pressure for 40 min. Lock the lid on the Ninja Foodi Multi-cooker and then cook for 40 min

4. To get 40 min' cook time, press *Pressure* button and use the Time Adjustment button to adjust the cook time to 40 min.

5. Pressure Release. Let the pressure to come down naturally for at least 14 to 16 min, then quick release any pressure left in the pot

6. Finish the dish. Close crisping lid and select Broil, set time to 7 min.

7. Transfer the chops, carrots and garlic cloves to a large serving bowl. Skim the fat off the sauce and ladle it over the servings.

BBQ Pulled Beef Sandwiches

Prep + Cooking Time: 1 hour, Serves: 2 to 4
Ingredients
- 2 lb. Beef of choice
- 4 cups finely shredded Cabbage the secret ingredient and you'll never know it's in there.
- 2 cups Water
- 1/2 cup of your favorite BBQ Sauce
- 1 cup Ketchup
- 1/3 cup Worcestershire Sauce
- 1 tbsp. mustard
- 1 tbsp. Horse Radish

Directions
1. Add and stir in ingredients to your Ninja Foodi Multi-cooker.
2. High pressure for 35 min. Lock the lid on the Ninja Foodi Multi-cooker and then cook for 35 min.
3. To get 35 min' cook time, press *Pressure* button and adjust the time.
4. Pressure Release. Use natural release method. Finish the dish. Remove the lid from the Ninja Foodi Multi-cooker. Close crisping lid. Select *Air Crisp*, set temperature to 390°F and set time to 15 min

5. Check after 10 min, cooking for an additional 5 min if dish needs more browning

6. Set the beef aside. Set the Ninja Foodi Multi-cooker to a *Sauté* mode, Sauté the sauce until it reaches the desired consistency. Serve and Enjoy.

Mouthwatering Beef Stew

Prep + Cooking Time: 1 hour 20 min, Serves: 4
Ingredients
- 1 ½ lb. lean ground beef about 93% lean
- 1 large sweet potato about 1 lb., peeled and shredded through the large holes of a box grater
- 1 tbsp. olive oil
- 1 large yellow onion, chopped.
- 1 tsp. ground cinnamon
- 1 tsp. ground cumin
- 1/2 tsp. dried sage
- 1/2 tsp. dried oregano
- 2 ½ cups beef broth
- 2 tbsp. yellow cornmeal
- 2 tbsp. honey
- 1/2 tsp. salt
- 1/2 tsp. ground black pepper

Directions
1. Heat the oil in the Ninja Foodi Multi-cooker turned to the Sauté function. Crumble in the ground beef; cook, stirring occasionally, until it loses its raw color and browns a bit, about 5 min
2. Add the onion; cook, often stirring, until softened, about 3 min
3. Stir in the sweet potato, cinnamon, cumin, sage, oregano, salt and pepper.
4. Cook for 1 minute, stirring constantly. Stir in the cornmeal and honey; cook for 1 minute, often stirring, to dissolve the cornmeal. Stir in the broth
5. High pressure for 5 min. Lock the lid on the Ninja Foodi Multi-cooker and then cook for 5 min.
6. To get 5 min' cook time, press *Pressure* button and use the Time Adjustment button to adjust the cook time to 5 min.
7. Pressure Release. Use the quick release method to drop the pot's pressure to normal.
8. Finish the dish. Remove the lid from the Ninja Foodi Multi-cooker. Close crisping lid. Select *Air Crisp*, set temperature to 390°F and set time to 20 min

9. Check after 15 min, cooking for an additional 15 min if dish needs more browning. Stir well and set aside, loosely covered, for 5 min before serving

Herbed Beef

Prep + Cooking Time: 25 min, Serves: 2
Ingredients
- 1 lb. beef fillets, cut into strips
- 1 yellow onion; chopped.
- 1 green bell pepper, cut into strips
- ½ tbsp. mustard
- 1 tbsp. olive oil
- 2 tsp. Provencal herbs
- Salt and black pepper to the taste

Directions
1. Set the Foodi on Sauté mode, add the oil and heat it up. Add the onion and the bell pepper, stir and cook for 5 min
2. Add the herbes, salt, pepper, the beef and the mustard, toss, put the pressure lid on and cook on High for 10 min. Release the pressure naturally for 10 min, divide everything into bowls and serve

Oregano Meatballs

Prep + Cooking Time: 30 min, Serves: 6
Ingredients
- 1 lb. pork meat; minced.
- 1 cup tomato puree
- ½ tbsp. lime peel; grated.
- 1 tbsp. oregano; chopped.
- 1 tbsp. bread crumbs
- 2 tbsp. parmesan; grated.
- Salt and black pepper to the taste

Directions
1. In a bowl mix all the ingredients except the tomato puree, stir well and shape medium meatballs out of this mix. Set the Foodi on Sauté mode, add the meatballs and brown them for 3 min
2. Add the tomato puree, toss a bit, put the pressure lid on and cook on High for 15 min. Release the pressure naturally for 10 min, divide the meatballs into bowls and serve as an appetizer.

Beef Roast

Prep + Cooking Time: 40 min, Serves: 4
Ingredients
- 1 lb. beef roast meat; cubed.
- 1 ½ cups chicken stock
- 2 garlic cloves; minced.
- 1 yellow onion; chopped.
- 3 tbsp. olive oil
- 1 tsp. thyme; chopped.
- Salt and black pepper to the taste

Directions
1. In your Foodi's baking pan, combine all the ingredients and toss them. Put the reversible rack in the machine, add the baking pan, set the pot on Roast mode and cook at 390 °F for 30 min. Divide between plates and serve right away

Chinese Pork

Prep + Cooking Time: 90 min, Serves: 8
Ingredients
- 3 lbs. pork shoulder roast
- 4 garlic cloves; minced.
- ¼ cup ketchup
- ¼ cup soy sauce
- ½ cup chicken stock
- ½ cup hoisin sauce
- ½ cup honey
- 1 tsp. Chinese five spice powder
- 4 tsp. ginger; grated.

Directions
1. Combine all the ingredients in the Foodi machine, put the pressure lid on and cook on High for 1 hour and 20 min. Release the pressure naturally for 10 min, divide everything between plates and serve

Delicious Pulled Pork Sandwiches

Prep + Cooking Time: 60 min, Serves: 8
Ingredients
- 2 ½ – 3 lb. uncooked boneless pork shoulder, cut in 1-inch cubes
- 1 can 6-ounces tomato paste
- 2 tbsp. barbecue seasoning
- 1 cup apple cider vinegar
- 1 tbsp. garlic powder

- 2 tsp. kosher salt
- Coleslaw and Potato rolls for servings

Directions

1. Add pork, spices, and vinegar to the pot. Assemble pressure lid, making sure the pressure release valve is in the SEAL position. Select PRESSURE and set to HIGH. Set time to 35 min. Select START/STOP to begin
2. When pressure cooking is complete, quick release the pressure by turning the pressure release valve to VENT position. Carefully remove lid when unit has finished releasing pressure.
3. Select SEAR/SAUTÉ and set to MEDIUM-HIGH. Select START/STOP to begin
4. Add tomato paste and stir to incorporate. Allow pork to simmer for 10 min, or until the liquid has reduced by half, as shown above, stirring occasionally with a wooden spoon or silicone tongs to shred the pork.
5. Serve pulled pork on potato rolls topped with coleslaw.

Honey Mustard Pork Tenderloin Recipe

Prep + Cooking Time: 30 min, Serves: 4

Ingredients

- 2 lbs. Pork Tenderloin
- 1 tbsp. Worcestershire Sauce
- 1/2 tbsp. Cornstarch
- 1/2 cup Chicken Broth
- 1/4 cup Balsamic Vinegar
- 1 clove Garlic, minced
- 2 tbsps. Olive Oil
- 1/4 cup Honey
- 1 tsp. Sage Powder
- 1 tbsp. Dijon Mustard
- 4 tbsp. Water
- Salt and Black Pepper to taste
- Brussels sprouts, sautéed

Directions

1. Put the pork on a clean flat surface and pat dry using paper towels. Season with salt and pepper. Select Sear/Sauté mode.
2. Heat the oil and brown the pork on both sides, for about 4 min in total. Remove the pork onto a plate and set aside
3. Add in honey, chicken broth, balsamic vinegar, garlic, Worcestershire sauce, mustard, and sage powder. Stir the ingredients and return the pork to the pot
4. Close the lid, secure the pressure valve, and select Pressure mode on High for 15 min. Once the timer has ended, do a quick pressure release. Remove the pork with tongs onto a plate and wrap it in aluminum foil
5. Next, mix the cornstarch with water and pour it into the pot. Select Sear/Sauté mode, stir the mixture and cook until it thickens. Then, turn the pot off after the desired thickness is achieved.
6. Unwrap the pork and use a knife to slice it with 3 to 4-inch thickness. Arrange the slices on a serving platter and spoon the sauce all over it. Serve with a syrupy sautéed Brussels sprouts.

Classic Brisket with Veggies

Prep + Cooking Time: 1 hour 20 min, Serves: 4 to 6

Ingredients

- 2 lb. or larger regular brisket, rinsed and patted dry
- 2 ½ cup homemade beef broth or make from Knorr Beef Base
- 2 tbsp. olive oil
- 5 or 6 red potatoes
- 2 cup large chunks carrots
- 3 tbsp. Worcestershire Sauce
- 4 bay leaves
- Granulated garlic
- Knorr Demi-Glace sauce
- 1/2 cup dehydrated onion
- 2 stalks celery in 1 chunks
- Fresh ground black pepper
- 3 tbsp. heaping chopped garlic
- 1 large yellow onion
- 5 or 6 red potatoes

Directions

1. Put the Ninja Foodi Multi-cooker on the sauté setting. Put in 1 tbsp. more if needed of the oil and caramelize the onions. Once golden, remove from pot, put in a bowl and set aside. But keep the Ninja Foodi Multi-cooker on the *Sauté* setting.
2. Rub the freshly ground pepper on both sides of the brisket. Do the same with the granulated garlic.

Add 1 tbsp. olive oil or more and only lightly sear the brisket on all sides

3. Add back the onions, garlic, Worcestershire sauce, bay leaves, dehydrated onion and beef broth
4. High pressure for 50 min. Close the lid and the pressure valve and then cook for 50 min
5. To get 50 min' cook time, press *Pressure* button and use the Time Adjustment button to adjust the cook time to 50 min
6. While the meat is cooking, peel and cut up all the veggies. When the meat is done, use the quick pressure release feature and then remove the lid. Add all of the veggies, replace the lid and cook at high pressure for to 10 min.
7. To get 10 min' cook time, press *Steam* button
8. Pressure Release. When the time is up, turn the pot off, use the quick release again and remove the lid.
9. Finish the dish. Close crisping lid. Select ""BROIL"" and set time to 8 min. Check after 5 min, cooking for an additional 3 min if dish needs more browning
10. Use a platter to remove the veggies and meat. Use the *Sauté* setting and bring the broth to a boil, then add the Knorr Demi-Glace mixing with a Wisk
11. Adjust seasonings as needed. Serve with Cole Slaw or other salad, homemade rolls or Italian garlic bread. Be sure to remove the bay leaves before serving. Serve and Enjoy

BBQ Pork with Ginger Coconut and Sweet Potatoes

Prep + Cooking Time: 40 min, Serves: 4
Ingredients
- 4 frozen uncooked boneless pork chops 8-ounces each
- 3 sweet potatoes, peeled, cut in 1-inch cubes
- 1/2 cup unsweetened coconut milk
- 1 tsp. Chinese five spice powder
- 1/2 stick 1/4 cup butter
- 1 tbsp. fresh ginger, peeled, minced
- 1/4 cup hoisin sauce
- 1/3 cup honey
- 1 ½ tbsp. soy sauce
- 1 tsp. kosher salt
- 1/2 tsp. white pepper

Directions
1. Place sweet potatoes and coconut milk into the pot. Place reversible rack inside pot over sweet potatoes, making sure rack is in the higher position.
2. Place pork chops on rack. Assemble pressure lid, making sure the PRESSURE RELEASE valve is in the SEAL position. Select PRESSURE and set to HIGH. Set time to 4 min. Select START/STOP to begin.
3. While pork chops and sweet potatoes are cooking, whisk together hoisin sauce, honey, soy sauce, and Chinese five spice powder.
4. When pressure cooking is complete, quick release the pressure by moving the PRESSURE RELEASE valve to the VENT position. Carefully remove lid when unit has finished releasing pressure
5. Remove rack with pork from pot. Mash sweet potatoes with butter, ginger, and salt, using a mashing utensil that won't scratch the nonstick surface of the pot
6. Place rack with pork back in pot and brush top of pork generously with 1/2 of sauce mixture.
7. Close crisping lid. Select BROIL and set time to 15 min. Select START/STOP to begin. After 5 min, open lid, flip pork chops, then brush them with remaining sauce.
8. Close lid to resume cooking. Check after 10 min and remove if desired doneness is achieved. If not, cook up to 5 more min, checking frequently. When cooking is complete, remove pork from rack and allow to rest for 5 min before serving with mashed potatoes

Delightful Lamb Shanks with Pancetta

Prep + Cooking Time: 1 hour 55 min, Serves: 4
Ingredients
- 1 28-ounce can diced tomatoes, drained about 3 ½ cups
- 4 12-ounce lamb shanks
- 1 6-ounce pancetta chunk, chopped.
- 2 cups dry, light white wine, such as Sauvignon Blanc
- 1-ounce dried mushrooms, preferably porcini, crumbled

- 2 tbsp. olive oil
- 1 small yellow onion, chopped.
- 3 tbsp. packed celery leaves, minced
- 2 tbsp. minced chives
- 2 tbsp. all-purpose flour
- 1/2 tsp. ground black pepper

Directions

1. Heat the oil in the Ninja Foodi Multi-cooker, turned to the *Sauté* function. Add the pancetta and brown well, about 6 min, stirring often. Use a slotted spoon to transfer the pancetta to a large bowl
2. Add two of the shanks to the cooker; brown on all sides, turning occasionally, about 8 min. Transfer them to the bowl and repeat with the remaining shanks.
3. Add the onion to the pot; cook, often stirring, until softened, about 4 min. Stir in the tomatoes, dried mushroom crumbles, celery leaves and chives. Cook until bubbling, about min, stirring often
4. Whisk the wine, flour and pepper in a medium bowl until the flour dissolves; stir this mixture into the sauce in the pot. Cook until thickened and bubbling, about 1 minute
5. Return the shanks, pancetta and their juices to the cooker.
6. High pressure for 60 min. Close the lid and the pressure valve and then cook for 60 min
7. To get 60 min' cook time, press *Pressure* button and use the Time Adjustment button to adjust the cook time to 60 min
8. Turn off the Ninja Foodi Multi-cooker or unplug it, so it doesn't jump to its keep-warm setting
9. Pressure Release. Let its pressure return to normal naturally, 20 to 30 min
10. Finish the dish. Remove the lid from the Ninja Foodi Multi-cooker. Close crisping lid. Select *Air Crisp*, set temperature to 375°F and set time to 18 min. Check after 10 min, cooking for an additional 8 min if dish needs more browning.
11. Transfer a shank to each serving bowl. Skim any surface fat from the sauce with a flatware spoon. Ladle the sauce and vegetables over the lamb shanks

Cinnamon Pork

Prep + Cooking Time: 30 min, Serves: 4

Ingredients

- 1 lb. pork stew meat; cubed.
- 1 yellow onion; chopped.
- 1 garlic clove; minced.
- 2 tbsp. olive oil
- 3 tbsp. parsley; chopped.
- 1 tsp. cinnamon powder
- Salt and black pepper to the taste

Directions

1. Set the Foodi on Sauté mode, add the oil and heat it up. Add the onion, stir and sauté for 5 min. Add the meat, garlic, cinnamon, salt and pepper, toss and sauté for 4-5 min more
2. Add the parsley, put the pressure lid on and cook on High for 12 min more. Release pre pressure naturally for 10 min, divide everything into bowls and serve

Special Biscuits

Prep + Cooking Time: 40 min, Serves: 6

Ingredients

- 12 oz. pork sausage, crumbled
- 16 oz. biscuit dough
- ½ cup cheddar cheese, shredded
- 3 cups milk
- ¼ cup white flour
- 2 tbsp. butter
- A pinch of salt and black pepper

Directions

1. Set the Foodi on Sauté mode, heat it up, add the sausage, salt and pepper, stir and cook for 5 min. Add the butter, milk and the flour, whisk well and cook for 7 min.
2. Meanwhile, separate each biscuit and fill each with the cheddar cheese. Put the reversible rack in the Foodi, place the biscuits in on the rack and lower it into the gravy
3. Set the machine on Baking mode and cook the biscuits at 325 °F for 15 min. Divide the biscuits between plates, drizzle the gravy all over and serve as a side.

Lamb and Eggplant Casserole

Prep + Cooking Time: 23 min, Serves: 4

Ingredients
- 1 ½ lb. lean ground lamb
- 1 small eggplant about 3/4 lb., stemmed and diced
- 8-ounces dried spiral-shaped pasta, such as rotini
- 1 tbsp. minced garlic
- 2 tbsp. olive oil
- 1 medium red onion, chopped.
- 1/2 cup canned tomato paste
- 3/4 cup dry red wine, such as Syrah
- 2 ¼ cups chicken broth
- 1/2 tbsp. dried oregano
- 1/2 tsp. dried dill
- 1 tsp. ground cinnamon
- 1/2 tsp. salt
- 1/2 tsp. ground black pepper

Directions

1. Heat the oil in the Ninja Foodi Multi-cooker turned to the *Sauté* function. Add the onion and cook, often stirring, until softened, about 4 min. Add the garlic and cook until aromatic, less than 1 minute.
2. Crumble in the ground lamb; cook, stirring occasionally until it has lost its raw color, about 5 min. Add the eggplant and cook for 1 minute, often stirring, to soften a bit. Pour in the red wine and scrape up any browned bits in the pot as it comes to a simmer
3. Stir in the broth, tomato paste, cinnamon, oregano, dill, salt and pepper until everything is coated in the tomato sauce. Stir in the pasta until coated.
4. High pressure for 8 min. Lock the lid on the Ninja Foodi Multi-cooker and then cook for 8 min.
5. To get 8 min' cook time, press *Pressure* button and use the Time Adjustment button to adjust the cook time to 8 min
6. Pressure Release. Use the quick release method.
7. Remove the lid from the Ninja Foodi Multi-cooker. Close crisping lid. Select "BROIL" and set time to 5 min. Cooking for an additional 4 min if dish needs more browning. Unlock and open the pot. Stir well before serving

Pork Loin and Apples

Prep + Cooking Time: 43 min, Serves: 8

Ingredients
- 1 3 lb. boneless pork loin roast
- 1 large red onion, halved and thinly sliced
- 2 medium tart green apples, such as Granny Smith, peeled, cored and thinly sliced
- 1/2 cup moderately sweet white wine, such as Riesling
- 2 tbsp. unsalted butter
- 1/4 cup chicken broth
- 4 fresh thyme sprigs
- 2 bay leaves
- 1/2 tsp. salt
- 1/2 tsp. ground black pepper

Directions

1. Melt the butter in the Ninja Foodi Multi-cooker, set on the *Sauté* function. Add the pork loin and brown it on all sides, turning occasionally, about 8 min in all. Transfer to a large plate.
2. Add the onion to the pot; cook, often stirring, until softened, about 3 min. Stir in the apple, thyme and bay leaves. Pour in the wine and scrape up any browned bits on the bottom of the pot
3. Pour in the broth; stir in the salt and pepper. Nestle the pork loin into this apple mixture; pour any juices from the plate into the pot.
4. High pressure for 30 min. Lock the lid on the Ninja Foodi Multi-cooker and then cook for 30 min.
5. To get 30 min' cook time, press *Pressure* button and adjust the time
6. Pressure Release. Use the quick release method to bring the pot's pressure to normal
7. Finish the dish. Close crisping lid and select Broil, set time to 7 min.
8. Transfer the pork to a cutting board; let stand for 5 min while you dish the sauce into serving bowls or onto a serving platter. Slice the loin into 1/2-inch-thick rounds and lay these over the sauce.

Beef Bites

Prep + Cooking Time: 20 min, Serves: 8
Ingredients
- 1 lb. beef meat, ground
- 1 egg; whisked.
- 1 yellow onion; chopped.
- 3 tbsp. breadcrumbs
- ½ tsp. garlic; minced.
- Cooking spray
- Salt and black pepper to the taste

Directions
1. In a bowl mix all the ingredients except the cooking spray, stir well and shape medium meatballs out of this mix
2. Put the meatballs in the Air Crisp basket, grease them with cooking spray, put the basket in the Foodi, set the machine on Air Crisp and cook the meatballs at 390 °F for 15 min. Serve the meatballs as an appetizer.

Paprika Pork Chops

Prep + Cooking Time: 25 min, Serves: 6
Ingredients
- 4 medium pork chops
- 2 garlic cloves; minced.
- ¼ cup olive oil
- 1 tbsp. sweet paprika
- Salt and black pepper to the taste

Directions
1. In a bowl mix the all the ingredients and toss. Put the pork chops in the Foodi's basket, set the machine on Air Crisp and cook at 400 °F for 15 min. Divide the chops between plates and serve.

Pork Carnitas

Prep + Cooking Time: 55 min, Serves: 4
Ingredients
- 2 lbs. pork butt; cubed.
- 1 yellow onion; chopped.
- 6 garlic cloves; minced.
- ½ cup chicken stock
- Juice of 1 orange
- A pinch of salt and black pepper
- ½ tsp. oregano, dried
- ½ tsp. cumin, ground

Directions
1. Put all the ingredients in the Ninja Foodi machine, put the pressure lid on and cook on High for 20 min.
2. Release the pressure fast for 4 min, set the machine on Sauté mode and cook everything for 15 min more. Set the Foodi on Broil mode, cook everything for 8 more min. Divide everything into bowls and serve

Pork Meatballs

Prep + Cooking Time: 25 min, Serves: 12
Ingredients
- 1 lb. pork meat, ground
- 2 garlic cloves; minced.
- ½ cup bread crumbs
- 2 cups sweet and sour sauce
- ½ cup pineapple; chopped.
- 1 cup scallions; chopped.
- 1 egg; whisked.
- 1 tbsp. ginger; grated.
- 1 tbsp. mustard
- 2 tbsp. soy sauce
- 1 tsp. coriander, ground
- Juice of 1 lime

Directions
1. In a bowl combine all the ingredients except the sauce, stir well and shape medium meatballs out of this mix
2. Put the meatballs in your Foodi, add the sweet and sour sauce, toss gently, put the pressure lid on and cook the meatballs on High for 15 min. Release the pressure naturally for 10 min, divide the meatballs into bowls and serve

Smoked Pork

Prep + Cooking Time: 40 min, Serves: 6
Ingredients
- 2 and ½ lbs. pork loin, boneless and cubed
- ¾ cup beef stock
- 1 tbsp. smoked paprika
- 2 tbsp. olive oil
- ½ tbsp. garlic powder
- 1 tsp. oregano, dried
- 1 tsp. basil, dried
- Salt and black pepper to the taste

Directions

1. In your Foodi's baking pan, combine all the ingredients and toss. Put the reversible rack in the machine, add the baking pan, set the pot on Roast mode and cook at 370 °F for 30 min. Divide everything between plates and serve

Pork Chops

Prep + Cooking Time: 25 min, Serves: 4

Ingredients
- 2 lbs. pork chops, boneless
- 1 green cabbage head, shredded
- 2 cups chicken stock
- A pinch of salt and black pepper
- 2 tbsp. butter, melted

Directions

1. Put all the ingredients in the Foodi machine, put the pressure lid on and cook on High for 15 min. Release the pressure naturally for 10 min, divide everything between plates and serve

Amazing Pork Chops with Applesauce

Prep + Cooking Time: 50 min, Serves: 4

Ingredients
- 2 to 4 pork loin chops we used center cut, bone-on
- 2 gala apples, thinly sliced
- 1 tsp. cinnamon powder
- 1 tbsp. honey
- 1/2 cup unsalted homemade chicken stock or water
- 1 tbsp. grapeseed oil or olive oil
- 1 small onion, sliced
- 3 cloves garlic, roughly minced
- 2 tbsp. light soy sauce
- 1 tbsp. butter
- Kosher salt and ground black pepper to taste
- 2 pieces whole cloves optional
- 1 ½ tbsp. cornstarch mixed with 2 tbsp. water optional

Directions

1. Make a few small cut around the sides of the pork chops so they will stay flat and brown evenly
2. Season the pork chops with a generous amount of kosher salt and ground black pepper.
3. Heat up your Ninja Foodi Multi-cooker. Add grapeseed oil into the pot. Add the seasoned pork chops into the pot, then let it brown for roughly 2 – 3 min on each side. Remove and set aside.
4. Add the sliced onions and stir. Add a pinch of kosher salt and ground black pepper to season if you like. Cook the onions for roughly 1 minute until softened. Then, add garlic and stir for 30 seconds until fragrance
5. Add in the thinly sliced gala apples, whole cloves optional and cinnamon powder, then give it a quick stir. Add the honey and partially deglaze the bottom of the pot with a wooden spoon
6. Add chicken stock and light soy sauce, then fully deglaze the bottom of the pot with a wooden spoon. Taste the seasoning and add more salt and pepper if desired
7. Place the pork chops back with all the meat juice into the pot
8. High pressure for 10 min. Lock the lid on the Ninja Foodi Multi-cooker and then cook for 10 min.
9. To get 10 min' cook time, press *Pressure* button and use the Time Adjustment button to adjust the cook time to 10 min
10. Pressure Release. Let it fully natural release roughly 10 min. Open the lid carefully.
11. Finish the dish. Close crisping lid. Select *Air Crisp*, set temperature to 375°F and set time to 10 min. Check after 10 min, cooking for an additional 5 min if dish needs more browning
12. Remove the pork chops and set aside. Turn the Multi-cooker to the Sauté setting. Remove the cloves and taste the seasoning one more time.
13. Add more salt and pepper if desired. Add butter and stir until it has fully dissolved into the sauce
14. Mix the cornstarch with water and mix it into the applesauce one third at a time until desired thickness.
15. Drizzle the applesauce over the pork chops and serve immediately with side dishes!

Simple Spare Ribs with Wine

Prep + Cooking Time: 75 min, Serves: 4

Ingredients
- 1 lb. pork spare ribs, cut into pieces
- 1 tbsp. corn starch
- 1 tbsp. olive oil
- 1 – 2 tsp. water
- Green onions as garnish
- 1 tsp. fish sauce optional

Black Bean Marinade:
- 3 cloves garlic, minced
- 1 tsp. sesame oil
- 1 tsp. sugar
- 1 tbsp. ginger, grated
- 1 tbsp. black bean sauce
- 1 tbsp. light soy sauce
- A pinch of white pepper

Directions

1. Marinate the pork spare ribs with Black Bean Marinade in an oven-safe bowl. Then, sit it in the fridge for 25 min.
2. First, mix 1 tbsp. of olive oil into the marinated spare ribs. Then, add 1 tbsp. of cornstarch and mix well. Finally, add 1 – 2 tsp. of water into the spare ribs and mix well
3. Add 1 cup of water into the Ninja Foodi Multi-cooker. Place steam rack in the Ninja Foodi Multi-cooker. Then, put the bowl of spare ribs on the rack
4. High pressure for 15 min. Lock the lid on the Ninja Foodi Multi-cooker and then cook for 15 min.
5. To get 15 min' cook time, press *Pressure* Button and then adjust the time
6. Pressure Release. Let the pressure to come down naturally for at least 15 min, then quick release any pressure left in the pot.
7. Finish the dish. Close crisping lid. Select *Air Crisp*, set temperature to 375°F and set time to 10 min. Check after 5 min, cooking for an additional 5 min if dish needs more browning
8. Taste and add one tsp. of fish sauce and green onions as garnish if you like. Serve immediately.

Yummy Pork Chops

Prep + Cooking Time: 35 min, Serves: 6

Ingredients
- 1 lb. pork chops
- 3 cups chicken stock
- 1 garlic clove; minced.
- 1 ½ cups heavy cream
- 2 yellow onions; chopped.
- 1 tbsp. olive oil
- 2 tbsp. sweet paprika
- 2 tbsp. dill; chopped.
- Salt and black pepper to the taste

Directions

1. Put the pork chops in your Foodi's basket, season with salt, pepper, garlic and the paprika, rub, set the machine on Air Crisp and cook at 380 °F for 10 min. Transfer the pork chops to the Foodi's baking pan, add all the other ingredients and toss
2. Place the baking pan in the machine, set it on Baking mode and cook at 370 °F for 15 min more. Divide everything between plates and serve hot

Garlic Pork Chops

Prep + Cooking Time: 30 min, Serves: 4

Ingredients
- 4 pork chops
- 4 garlic cloves; minced.
- 2 tbsp. rosemary; chopped.
- 2 tbsp. olive oil
- Salt and black pepper to the taste

Directions

1. In a bowl mix all the ingredients and toss them well. Put the reversible rack in the Foodi and add the basket inside
2. Add the pork chops to the basket, set the machine on Air Crisp and cook at 400 °F for 20 min. Serve with a side salad.

Ninja Pulled Pork

Prep + Cooking Time: 2 hour 5 min, Serves: 10

Ingredients
- 1 4- to 4½ lb. bone in skinless pork shoulder, preferably pork butt
- Up to 1 ½ cups light-colored beer, preferably a pale ale or amber lager
- 1/2 tsp. garlic powder
- 1/2 tsp. ground cloves
- 1/2 tsp. ground cinnamon

- 2 tbsp. smoked paprika
- 2 tbsp. packed dark brown sugar
- 1 tbsp. ground cumin
- 1/2 tbsp. dry mustard
- 1 tsp. ground coriander
- 1 tsp. dried thyme
- 1 tsp. onion powder
- 1 tsp. salt
- 2 tsp. ground black pepper

Directions
1. Mix the smoked paprika, brown sugar, cumin, pepper, mustard, coriander, thyme, onion powder, salt, garlic powder, cloves and cinnamon in a small bowl. Massage the mixture all over the pork.
2. Set the pork in the Ninja Foodi Multi-cooker. Pour 1cup beer into the electric cooker without knocking the spices off the meat
3. High pressure for 80 min. Lock the lid on the Ninja Foodi Multi-cooker and then cook for 80 min.
4. To get 80 min' cook time, press *Pressure* button and use the Time Adjustment button to adjust the cook time to 80 min.
5. Pressure Release. Let its pressure fall to normal naturally, 25 to 35 min
6. Finish the dish. Close crisping lid and select Broil, set time to 7 min
7. Transfer the meat to a large cutting board. Let stand for 5 min. Use a spoon to skim as much fat off the sauce in the pot as possible
8. Set the *Sauté* function. Bring the sauce to a simmer, stirring occasionally; continue boiling the sauce, often stirring, until reduced by half, 7 to 10 min.
9. Use two forks to shred the meat off the bones; discard the bones and any attached cartilage. Pull any large chunks of meat apart with the forks and stir the meat back into the simmering sauce to reheat. Serve and Enjoy!

Rosemary Sausage and Onion

Prep + Cooking Time: 35 min, Serves: 4
Ingredients
- 6 pork sausage links, halved
- 2 yellow onion, sliced
- 2 garlic cloves; minced.
- 1 tbsp. rosemary; chopped.
- 1 tbsp. olive oil
- 1 tbsp. sweet paprika
- Salt and black pepper to the taste

Directions
1. In your Foodi's baking pan, combine all the ingredients and toss. Put the reversible rack in the Foodi, add the baking pan, set the machine on Baking mode and cook at 370 °F for 25 min. Divide between plates and serve

Peppers and Pork Stew

Prep + Cooking Time: 30 min, Serves: 4
Ingredients
- 1 large yellow or white onion, chopped.
- 1 large green bell pepper, stemmed, cored and cut into 1/4-inch-thick strips
- 1 lb. boneless center-cut pork loin chops, cut into 1/4-inch-thick strips
- 1 large red bell pepper, stemmed, cored and cut into 1/4-inch-thick strips
- 1 14-ounce can diced tomatoes, drained about 1 3/4 cups
- 2 tsp. minced, seeded fresh jalapeño chile
- 2 tsp. dried oregano
- 2 tbsp. olive oil
- 2 tsp. minced garlic
- 2 ½ cups canned hominy drained and rinsed
- 1 cup chicken broth

Directions
1. Heat the oil in a Ninja Foodi Multi-cooker, turned to the Sauté function. Add the onion and both bell peppers; cook, often stirring, until the onion softens, about 4 min.
2. Add the garlic, jalapeño and oregano; stir well until aromatic, less than 20 seconds. Add the hominy, tomatoes, broth and pork; stir over the heat for 1 minute
3. High pressure for 12 min. Lock the lid on the Ninja Foodi Multi-cooker and then cook for 12 min.
4. To get 12 min' cook time, press *Pressure* button and use the Time Adjustment button to adjust the cook time to 12 min.
5. Pressure Release. Use the quick release method to bring the pot's pressure back to normal. Unlock and open the cooker. Stir well before serving

Buttery Pork Steaks

Prep + Cooking Time: 24 min, Serves: 4

Ingredients
- 4 pork steaks
- 2 tbsp. butter, melted
- 1 tbsp. smoked paprika
- Salt and black pepper to the taste

Directions

1. In a bowl mix all the ingredients and toss them. Put the steaks in the Foodi's basket, set the machine on Air Crisp and cook at 390 °F for 7 min on each side. Divide the steaks between plates and serve

Garlic Pork

Prep + Cooking Time: 35 min, Serves: 4

Ingredients
- 1 ½ lbs. pork stew meat; cubed.
- 1 tbsp. smoked paprika
- 3 tbsp. olive oil
- 3 tbsp. garlic; minced.
- Salt and black pepper to the taste

Directions

1. In the Foodi's baking pan, combine all the ingredients and toss. Put the reversible rack in the machine, add the baking pan inside, set the pot on Roast mode and cook at 390 °F for 25 min. Divide everything between plates and serve with a side salad

Chapter 3: Poultry Recipes

Best Butter Chicken

Time: 30 min, Serves: 4

Ingredients

- 2 tbsp of ghee
- 1 large yellow onion (finely diced)
- 2 pounds of boneless, skinless chicken thighs, halved and patted dry
- 1 cup of canned tomato puree
- 1/2 cup of water
- 1 tbsp of grated fresh ginger
- 1 tbsp of minced garlic
- 2 tsp of red chili powder
- 2 tsp of salt
- 1 tsp of garam masala
- 1/2 tsp of ground turmeric
- 1/2 cup of canned coconut cream
- 2 tbsp of tomato paste
- 2 tbsp of dried fenugreek leaves
- 2 tsp of brown sugar
- 1/2 cup of chopped fresh cilantro

Directions

1. In a large frying pan, heat the ghee. Add the onion and cook until it is translucent and shiny. This should take approximately 5 min. Add the chicken, tomato puree, water, ginger, garlic, chilli powder, salt, garam masala, and turmeric and stir to combine, then pour the mixture into your pressure cooker cooking pot.

2. Add to the pot the coconut cream, tomato paste, fenugreek, and brown sugar and stir to combine everything together.

3. Seal the lid of your pressure cooker, set the pressure to high and set the timer for 20 min. Once the timer is up, open the quick release valve in order to release the pressure from the pot carefully. Serve with rice or over pasta.

Cheesy Chicken and Bacon Chowder

Time: 30 min, Serves: 6

Ingredients

- 2 pounds of chicken breasts (boneless and skinless, chopped)
- 12 oz cream cheese block and a half (cubed)
- 2 1 oz packets of Dry Ranch Seasoning mix
- 8 oz bacon bits, cooked and chopped
- 1 cup of cheddar cheese
- 1 cup of chicken bone broth or water

Directions

1. Pour 1 cup of your bone broth or water into the bottom of your pressure cooker cooking pot.

2. Add the chopped chicken to your pressure cooker, and top with the cream cheese cubes and seasoning powder, then seal the lid.

3. Set the pressure cooker pressure to high and the timer for 12 min for chicken.

4. Once the timer is up, carefully use the quick release valve to remove the pressure from the pot.

5. Add the cheddar cheese and bacon bits to the cooked chicken chunks and mix the ingredients together until the cheese begins to melt.

6. Place the lid back on the pressure cooker (but don't turn it on, it will be hot enough to warm the bacon) for about 5 min. Letting the ingredients sit for a few min will also allow the sauce to thicken.

7. This can then be served with rice, pasta, or eaten as it is!

Chicken and Chimichuri

Prep + Cooking Time: 45 min, Serves: 2

Ingredients

- 2 chicken breasts, bone-in, skin-on
- 1 tbsp. olive oil
- 1 tbsp. fennel, ground
- 1 tbsp. chili powder
- 1 tbsp. sweet paprika
- 1 tsp. garlic powder
- 1 tsp. onion powder
- 1 tsp. cumin, ground
- A pinch of salt and black pepper

For the chimichuri:

- ¼ cup olive oil
- ½ bunch parsley
- 4 garlic cloves; minced.

- 1 shallot; chopped.
- ½ bunch cilantro
- Zest and juice of 1 lemon

Directions
1. In a bowl mix the paprika with salt, pepper, fennel, chili powder, garlic powder, onion powder, 1 tbsp. oil and the cumin and whisk well
2. Add the chicken breasts and toss them well. Put the basket in the Foodi, add the chicken, set the machine on Air Crisp mode and cook the meat at 375 °F for 35 min
3. In a blender, mix the cilantro with ¼ cup oil, parsley, the garlic, shallot, lemon zest and lemon juice and pulse well. Divide the chicken breasts between plates, top with the chimichuri and serve

Herbed Whole Roasted Chicken

Prep + Cooking Time: 50 min, Serves: 4
Ingredients
- 1 whole uncooked chicken 4 ½ - 5 lb.
- 1 tbsp. whole black peppercorns
- 2 tbsp. plus 2 tsp. kosher salt, divided.
- 1/4 cup hot water
- 1/4 cup honey
- Juice of 2 lemons 1/4 cup lemon juice
- 5 sprigs fresh thyme
- 5 cloves garlic, peeled, smashed
- 1 tbsp. canola oil
- 2 tsp. ground black pepper

Directions
1. Rinse chicken and tie legs together with cooking twine
2. In a small bowl, mix together lemon juice, hot water, honey, and 2 tbsp. salt. Pour mixture into the pot. Place whole peppercorns, thyme, and garlic in the pot.
3. Place chicken into the Cook & Crisp basket and place basket in pot. Assemble pressure lid, making sure the pressure release valve is in the SEAL position. Select PRESSURE and set to HIGH. Set time to 22 min. Select START/STOP to begin
4. When pressure cooking is complete, allow pressure to naturally release for 5 min. After 5 min, quick release remaining pressure by moving the pressure release valve to the VENT position. Carefully remove lid when unit has finished releasing pressure
5. Brush chicken with canola oil or spray with cooking spray. Season with salt and pepper.
6. Close crisping lid. Select AIR CRISP, set temperature to 400°F, and set time to 8 min. Select START/STOP to begin. Cook until desired level of crispness is reached, adding up to 10 additional min
7. Cooking is complete when internal temperature reaches 165°F. Remove chicken from basket using 2 large serving forks. Let rest for 5 to 10 min before serving

Turkey Breast

Prep + Cooking Time: 1 hour 10 min, Serves: 4
Ingredients
- 1 frozen turkey breast with frozen gravy packet
- 1 whole onion

Directions
1. Place frozen turkey breast, rozen gravy packet and whole onion in the Ninja Foodi Multi-cooker
2. High pressure for 30 min. Lock the lid on the Ninja Foodi Multi-cooker and then cook for 30 min.
3. To get 30 min' cook time, press *Pressure* button and use the Time Adjustment button to adjust the cook time to 30 min
4. Pressure Release. Use natural release method.
5. Remove lid, turn turkey breast over
6. High pressure for 30 min. Replace lid on the Ninja Foodi Multi-cooker and then cook for 30 min.
7. To get 30 min' cook time, press *Pressure* button
8. and use the Time Adjustment button to adjust the cook time to 30 min.
9. Pressure Release. Use natural release method, again.
10. Finish the dish. Close crisping lid. Select *Air Crisp*, set temperature to 360°F and set time to 10 min. Check after 5 min, cooking for an additional 5 min if dish needs more browning
11. Remove mesh. Remove turkey and slice. Places slices and turkey gravy into serving dish

Great Chicken Wings

Prep + Cooking Time: 35 min, Serves: 4

Ingredients
- 2 lbs. chicken wings
- 2 tbsp. buffalo sauce
- ½ cup water
- 2 tbsp. canola oil

Directions

1. Put the water in the Foodi, add the Air Crisp basket and put the wings in the basket. Put the pressure lid on, cook on High for 5 min, release the pressure naturally for 10 min and toss the wings with the oil

2. Set the machine on Air Crisp mode, cook the wings for 15 min more at 390 °F and transfer them to a bowl. Add the buffalo sauce, toss well and serve

Black Bean Soup

Prep + Cooking Time: 70 min, Serves: 6

Ingredients
- 2 yellow onions; chopped.
- 2 cups black beans
- 5 cups water
- 1 cup brewed coffee
- 1 cup sour cream
- Zest and juice of 1 lime
- 1 red bell pepper; chopped.
- 1 jalapeno pepper; chopped.
- 4 garlic cloves; minced.
- 2 bay leaves
- 2 celery stalks; chopped.
- 1 tbsp. tomato paste
- 3 tbsp. canola oil
- 1 tbsp. cumin, ground
- A pinch of salt and black pepper

Directions

1. Set the Foodi on Sauté mode, add the oil, heat it up, add onions, bay leaves, red bell pepper, garlic, celery, jalapeno, salt and pepper, stir and cook for 10 min

2. Add cumin, tomato paste, water, beans and coffee, stir, put the pressure lid on and cook on High for 50 min

3. Release the pressure naturally for 10 min, add the lime zest and lime juice, stir, divide the soup into bowls, top each serving with sour cream and serve.

Chicken and cashews

Time: 25 min, Serves: 2

Ingredients
- 2 chicken breasts (cut into cubes)
- 6 tbsp of soy sauce (low sodium works best)
- 3/4 tbsp of apple cider vinegar
- 2 tbsp of natural honey
- 1 tsp of toasted sesame oil
- 2 tbsp of olive oil
- 2 tsp of minced garlic
- 1/2 tsp of grated ginger
- 1 cup of green peppers (chopped)
- 1/2 cup of carrots (chopped)
- 1 1/2 cups Jasmine or Basmati rice (washed, rinsed and drained thoroughly)
- 1 cup of water
- 2/3 cup of roasted, unsalted cashews
- Chopped green onions for garnish
- A pinch of salt and pepper to taste

Directions

1. In a medium bowl, whisk together the soy sauce, vinegar, honey, and sesame oil then set aside.

2. Then in a large frying pan, heat the olive oil. When the oil is hot, add the chicken and season with salt and pepper. Sauté for 2-3 min, until lightly brown. Add the garlic and ginger and cook for another 20 seconds then remove from the heat.

3. Pour your cooked chicken and seasonings into your pressure cooker cooking pot, then pour in 1/2 of the sauce, your uncooked rice, the peppers, carrots and the 1 cup of water.

4. Seal the pressure cooker lid, then set the pressure to high, and set the timer for 5 min, then press start. When the timer is up, allow the pressure to naturally release for the next 10 min, then use the quick release valve to release any remaining pressure. Remove the lid carefully.

5. Sprinkle in cashews and green onions, and give the pot a final stir before serving.

Best BBQ and Honey Glazed Wings

Time: 30 min, Serves: 4

Ingredients

- 2 pounds of frozen chicken wings
- 1 cup of your favorite BBQ sauce
- 1/2 cup of brown sugar
- 2 tbsp Worcestershire sauce
- 1 tbsp fresh minced garlic
- 1/2 cup water
- 1/2 cup of honey
- ½ tsp ground cayenne pepper

Directions

1. Inside your pressure cooking pot add the water, honey, garlic, cayenne pepper, Worcestershire sauce, brown sugar and BBQ sauce. Mix all ingredients thoroughly, then add in the chicken wings and stir to coat them in sauce.

2. Seal the pressure cooker lid, set the pressure to high and set the timer for 15 min.

3. Once the wings are cooked and the timer is up, carefully use the quick release valve to release the pressure build up in the pot. Carefully open the lid and remove the wings using kitchen tongs.

4. Line a baking tray with aluminum foil and spread the cooked wings onto the tray, then pour extra sauce from the pressure cooker over the tops of the wings, and put them into the oven to grill on high heat for a further 5 min.

5. Serve in a large bowl with dips or other snacks.

Rosemary Turkey

Prep + Cooking Time: 60 min, Serves: 4

Ingredients

- 2 turkey breasts, skinless, boneless and halved
- 1 tbsp. lime juice
- 2 tbsp. olive oil
- 2 tsp. garlic powder
- 1 tsp. rosemary, dried
- Salt and black pepper to the taste

Directions

1. In a bowl mix all the ingredients and toss. Put the basket in the Foodi machine, put the turkey breasts in it, set the machine on Air Crisp and cook at 370 °F for 35 min, flipping the turkey halfway. Serve hot with a side salad

Stuffed Chicken Recipe

Prep + Cooking Time: 30 min, Serves: 4

Ingredients

- 4 Chicken Breasts, skinless
- 1 cup Baby Spinach, frozen
- 1/2 cup crumbled Feta Cheese
- 2 tbsp. Olive Oil
- 2 tsp dried Parsley
- 1/2 tsp dried Oregano
- 1/2 tsp Garlic Powder
- Salt and Black Pepper to taste
- 1 cup Water

Directions

1. Wrap the chicken in plastic and put on a cutting board. Use a rolling pin to pound flat to a quarter inch thickness. Remove the plastic wrap

2. In a bowl, mix spinach, salt, and feta cheese and scoop the mixture onto the chicken breasts. Wrap the chicken to secure the spinach filling in it

3. Use toothpicks to secure the wrap firmly from opening. Gently season the chicken pieces with oregano, parsley, garlic powder, and pepper.

4. Select Sear/Sauté mode on Foodi Ninja. Heat the oil, add the chicken, and sear to golden brown on each side. Work in 2 batches.

5. Remove the chicken onto a plate and set aside. Pour the water into the pot and use a spoon to scrape the bottom of the pot to let loose any chicken pieces or seasoning that is stuck to the bottom of the pot. Fit the reversible rack into the pot with care as the pot will still be hot

6. Transfer the chicken onto the rack. Seal the lid and select Pressure mode on High pressure for 10 min. Press Start/Stop.

7. Once the timer has ended, do a quick pressure release. Close the crisping lid and cook on Bake/Roast mode for 5 min at 370 F.

8. Plate the chicken and serve with a side of sautéed asparagus, and some slices of tomatoes

Easy Chicken Teriyaki

Time: 50 min, Serves: 4

Ingredients

- 8 chicken legs or thighs
- 1 medium onion (chopped)
- 1/2 cup of soy sauce
- 2 tbsp rice wine vinegar
- 1/4 cup of brown sugar
- 1 tbsp minced garlic
- 1 tbsp minced ginger
- 1/2 cup of bone broth or water
- 2 Green peppers (chopped)
- Sesame seeds for serving

Directions

1. In a large bowl, mix together your soy sauce, rice wine vinegar, brown sugar, garlic, and ginger to make the teriyaki sauce marinade. Add your chicken to your marinade and set aside for 30 min.
2. Once the chicken has had time to marinade, place the chicken pieces, onion, green peppers, marinade and bone broth or water into the cooking pot of your pressure cooker.
3. Seal the lid and set your pressure to high pressure, and the timer to 15 min, then press the start button.
4. Once the timer has finished, carefully use the quick release valve to release the pressure from your pot and gently open the lid.
5. Serve chicken immediately with some rice or noodles, and a sprinkle of sesame seeds.

Vegetable Stock Recipe

Prep + Cooking Time: 11 min, Serves: 6

Ingredients

- 2 large unpeeled yellow onions; sliced lengthwise in half, root ends removed
- 1 bunch fresh flat leaf parsley; tied with string so it's easy to remove
- 2 medium tomatoes fresh or canned
- 2 unpeeled garlic
- 2 medium carrots; snapped in half
- 2 celery stalks; snapped in half
- 1 tbsp. whole black peppercorns
- 2 bay leaves
- Cold water; as needed

Directions

1. Add the vegetables, herbs and spices to the Multi-cooker base. Pour in cold water to just cover these ingredients.
2. High pressure for 10 min. Lock the lid on the Ninja Foodi Multi-cooker and then cook for 10 min.
3. To get 10 min' cook time, press *Pressure* button and use the Time Adjustment button to adjust the cook time to 10 min
4. Pressure Release Let the pressure to come down naturally for at least 20 to 30 min, then quick release any pressure left in the pot.
5. Finish the dish. Carefully strain the contents of the cooker into a stainless steel bowl and let cool to room temperature. Reserve the solids or discard them. Freeze the stock if not using in the next couple of days

Creamy Asparagus Soup

Prep + Cooking Time: 11 min, Serves: 4

Ingredients

- 1 lb. asparagus; tough ends removed, cut into 1-inch pieces
- 3 green onions; sliced crosswise into 1/4-inch pieces
- 1 tbsp. olive oil
- 4 cups salt-free Chicken Stock
- 1 tsp. ground white pepper; plus more as needed
- 1/2 cup heavy cream
- 1 tbsp. unsalted butter
- 1 tbsp. all-purpose flour
- 2 tsp. salt

Directions

1. Heat the Ninja Foodi Multi-cooker using the *Sauté* function, add the oil, green onions and a pinch of salt. Sauté the green onions for a few min, then add the asparagus and stock
2. High pressure for 5 min. Lock the lid on the Ninja Foodi Multi-cooker and then cook for 5 min.
3. To get 5 min' cook time, press *Pressure* button and use the Time Adjustment button to adjust the cook time to 5 min.
4. Meanwhile, make a blond roux: In a small saucepan over low heat, mix the butter and flour

and cook, constantly stirring, until the butter has melted and the mixture foams and begins to turn golden beige. Remove from the heat.
5. Pressure Release. When the time is up, open the cooker with the Natural Release method
6. Finish the dish. Add the roux, salt and pepper to the soup and puree with an immersion blender until smooth. Taste and season with more pepper if you wish. Swirl in the cream just before serving. Serve and Enjoy!

Chicken and Tomatoes

Prep + Cooking Time: 25 min, Serves: 4
Ingredients
- 2 chicken breasts, skinless, boneless and cubed
- ¼ cup cheddar; grated.
- ½ cup tomatoes; chopped.
- ½ cup heavy cream
- ¾ cup chicken stock
- 2 garlic cloves; minced.
- 2 tbsp. basil; chopped.
- 1 tbsp. olive oil
- 1 tbsp. rosemary; chopped.
- 1 tsp. chili powder
- Salt and black pepper to the taste

Directions
1. Set the Foodi on Sauté mode, add the oil and heat it up. Add the garlic, tomatoes, rosemary, chili, salt and pepper, stir and cook for 5 min
2. Add all the other ingredients, toss, put the pressure lid on and cook on High for 15 min. Release the pressure naturally for 10 min, divide everything into bowls and serve

Chicken Stock Recipe

Prep + Cooking Time: 1 hour 10 min, Serves: 10 cups
Ingredients
- 2 ½ lb. chicken carcasses
- 2 carrots; diced
- 2 bay leaves
- 4 garlic cloves; crushed
- 1 tsp. whole peppercorn
- 2 celery stalks; diced
- 2 onions keep the outer layers too; diced
- 1 tbsp. apple cider vinegar optional
- 10 cups water
- Your favorite fresh herbs

Directions
1. Optional step: Brown the chicken carcasses in your Ninja Foodi Multi-cooker with 1 tbsp. of oil. This will slightly elevate the flavors and result in a brown stock. Then, add water to deglaze the pot with 1/2 Cup 100 ml of water
2. Add all ingredients in the Ninja Foodi Multi-cooker.
3. High pressure for 60 min. Lock the lid on the Ninja Foodi Multi-cooker and then cook for 60 min.
4. To get 60 min' cook time, press *Pressure* button and use the Time Adjustment button to adjust the cook time to 60 min.
5. Pressure Release. When the time is up, open the cooker with the Natural Release method
6. Finish the dish. Open the lid. Strain the stock through a colander discarding the solids and set aside to cool. Let the stock sit in the fridge until the fat rises to the top and form a layer of gel. Then, skim off the fat on the surface.
7. You can use the stock immediately, keep it in the fridge or freeze it for future use

Cumin Chicken Wings

Prep + Cooking Time: 30 min, Serves: 4
Ingredients
- 8 chicken wings, halved
- ¼ cup chicken stock
- 2 garlic cloves; minced.
- 1 tbsp. olive oil
- 2 tsp. cumin, ground
- Salt and black pepper to the taste

Directions
1. Put the chicken wings in the Foodi's basket, set the machine on Air Crisp and cook them at 360 °F for 10 min and transfer to a bowl
2. Clean the machine, set it on Sauté mode, add the oil and heat it up. Add the chicken wings and all the other ingredients, toss and cook everything for 10 more min

Rotisserie Chicken

Time: 1 hour, Serves: 4

Ingredients

- 1 whole chicken (3 to 4 pounds)
- 1 tsp of garlic powder
- 1 tsp of onion powder
- 1 tsp of ground paprika
- 1 tsp of dried thyme
- Pinch of salt and pepper to taste
- 1 lemon (sliced)
- 1 cup of water

Directions

1. In a small bowl, combine your salt, pepper, garlic powder, onion powder, paprika, and thyme. Then add your lemon slices to the spices and use the end of a rolling pin just to smack them a bit and release the juices.

2. Place your whole chicken into an oven roasting or crockpot bag, and pour the spice mix and lemon slices evenly over your chicken. Give it a good rub and massage the bag a bit before making a knot in the end. Poke a few holes into the top of the bag to allow the steam to escape while cooking.

3. Pour 1 cup of water into the bottom of your pressure cooker and put in your reversible wire rack above the water. Gently lower the chicken onto the rack and seal the pressure cooker lid.

4. Set the pressure of your pressure cooker to high, and set the timer for 45 min.

5. Once the chicken is cooked, allow the pressure to naturally release for 10 min, then use the quick release valve to release the remaining pressure.

6. Open the bag very carefully as the steam will burn. Serve immediately with salad or vegetables of your choice.

Chapter 4: Fish and Seafood Recipes

Fish & Fries

Prep time: 30 min, Serves: 4

Ingredients
- 1 lb. potatoes, sliced into strips
- 2 tablespoons olive oil
- Salt and pepper to taste
- 1/4 cup all purpose flour
- 1 egg
- 2 tablespoons water
- 2/3 cup cornflakes, crushed
- 1 tablespoon Parmesan cheese, grated
- 1 lb. cod fillets

Directions
1. Coat the potato strips with oil, salt and pepper. Place in the Ninja Foodi basket.
2. Seal the crisping lid and set it to air crisp.
3. Cook at 400 degrees F for 10 min, stirring halfway through.
4. While waiting, combine the flour with salt and pepper in one bowl.
5. In another bowl, beat the egg and add water.
6. In the third bowl, mix the cornflakes and Parmesan.
7. Dip each fillet in the flour mixture. Then dip into the second and third bowls.
8. Place in the Ninja Foodi basket. Seal the lid and choose air crisp function.
9. Cook at 400 degrees for 10 min.

Serving Suggestion: Serve with tartar sauce.
Tip: Sprinkle with salt and pepper before serving.
Nutrition value/serving: Calories 312, Total Fat 10.8g, Saturated Fat 2.4g, Cholesterol 101mg, Sodium 191mg, Total Carbohydrate 28.1g, Dietary Fiber 3.1g, Total Sugars 1.9g, Protein 26.7g, Potassium 493mg

Crispy Shrimp

Prep time: 20 min, Serves: 4

Ingredients
- 1 lb. shrimp, peeled and deveined
- 2 eggs
- 1/2 cup bread crumbs
- 1/2 cup onion, diced
- 1 teaspoon ginger
- 1 teaspoon garlic powder
- Salt and pepper to taste

Directions
1. In one bowl, beat the two eggs. In another bowl, put the rest of the ingredients.
2. Dip the shrimp first in the eggs and then in the spice mixture.
3. Place in the Ninja Foodi basket. Seal the crisping lid. Choose air crisp function.
4. Cook at 350 degrees for 10 min.

Serving Suggestion: Serve with chili sauce.
Tip: Keep the tails of the shrimp intact.
Nutrition value/serving: Calories 229, Total Fat 4.9g, Saturated Fat 1.4g, Cholesterol 321mg, Sodium 407mg, Total Carbohydrate 13.8g, Dietary Fiber 1.1g, Total Sugars 1.8g, Protein 30.7g, Potassium 283mg

Southern Fried Fish Fillet

Prep time: 30 min, Serves: 4

Ingredients
- 2 lb. white fish fillet
- 1 cup low fat milk
- 1 lemon slice
- 1/2 cup mustard
- 1/2 cup cornmeal
- 1/4 cup all purpose flour
- 2 tablespoons dried parsley flakes
- Salt and pepper to taste
- 1/4 teaspoon chili powder
- 1/4 teaspoon garlic powder
- 1/4 teaspoon onion powder
- 1/4 teaspoon cayenne pepper

Directions
1. Place the fish fillet in a bowl. Pour the milk over the fish fillet.
2. Squeeze lemon slice over the fish. Marinate for 15 min.
3. Spread the mustard on the fish fillets.
4. In another bowl, mix the rest of the ingredients.

5. Coat the fish fillets with the cornmeal mixture. Place on the Ninja Foodi basket.
6. Set it to air crisp. Seal the crisping lid. Cook at 390 degrees for 10 min.
7. Flip the fillets and cook for 5 more min.
Serving Suggestion: Serve with fresh green salad.
Tip: You can use Dijon mustard or yellow mustard for this recipe.
Nutrition value/serving: Calories 595, Total Fat 24g, Saturated Fat 3.4g, Cholesterol 178mg, Sodium 184mg, Total Carbohydrate 28.4g, Dietary Fiber 4.5g, Total Sugars 4.8g, Protein 64.7g, Potassium 1221mg

Ranch Fish Fillet

Prep time: 20 min, Serves: 4
Ingredients
- 3/4 cup bread crumbs
- 1 packet dry ranch dressing mix
- 2 1/2 tablespoons vegetable oil
- 2 eggs, beaten
- 4 fish fillets

Directions
1. Combine the bread crumbs and ranch mix in a bowl. Pour in the oil.
2. Dip each fish fillet into the egg and cover with the crumb mixture.
3. Place in the Ninja Foodi basket. Seal the lid. Select air crisp function.
4. Cook at 360 degrees F for 12 min, flipping halfway through.
Serving Suggestion: Garnish with lemon wedges.
Tip: For added flavor, season the fish with salt and pepper.
Nutrition value/serving: Calories 425, Total Fat 25.4g, Saturated Fat 5.7g, Cholesterol 113mg, Sodium 697mg, Total Carbohydrate 30.4g, Dietary Fiber 1.4g, Total Sugars 1.4g, Protein 18.8g, Potassium 360mg

Ranch Warm Fillets

Prep time: 5 min, Cooking time: 13 min, Serves: 4
Ingredients
- 1/4 cup panko
- 1/2 packet ranch dressing mix powder
- 1 and 1/4 tablespoons vegetable oil
- 1 egg beaten
- 2 tilapia fillets
- A garnish of herbs and chilies

Directions
1. Pre-heat your Ninja Foodi with the Crisping Basket inside at 350 degrees F
2. Take a bowl and mix in ranch dressing and panko
3. Beat eggs in a shallow bowl and keep it on the side
4. Dip fillets in the eggs, then in the panko mix
5. Place fillets in your Ninja Foodie's insert and transfer insert to Ninja Foodi
6. Lock Air Crisping Lid and Air Crisp for 13 min at 350 degrees F
7. Garnish with chilies and herbs. Enjoy!
Nutrition value/serving: Calories: 301, Fat: 12g, Carbohydrates: 1.5g, Protein: 28g

Tuna Patties

Prep time: 30 min, Serves: 2
Ingredients
- 2 cans tuna flakes
- 1/2 tablespoon almond flour
- 1 teaspoon dried dill
- 1 tablespoon mayo
- 1/2 teaspoon onion powder
- 1 teaspoon garlic powder
- Salt and pepper to taste
- 1 tablespoon lemon juice

Directions
1. Mix all the ingredients in a bowl. Form patties. Set the tuna patties on the Ninja Foodi basket. Seal the crisping lid. Set it to air crisp.
2. Cook at 400 degrees for 10 min. Flip and cook for 5 more min.
Serving Suggestion: Serve with fresh green salad.
Tip: Add more flour if too wet.
Nutrition value/serving: Calories 141, Total Fat 6.4g, Saturated Fat 0.7g, Cholesterol 17mg, Sodium 148mg, Total Carbohydrate 5.2g, Dietary Fiber 1g, Total Sugars 1.2g, Protein 17g, Potassium 48mg

Crispy Cod Fish

Prep time: 30 min, Serves: 4

Ingredients
- 4 cod fish fillets
- Salt and sugar to taste
- 1 teaspoon sesame oil
- 250 ml water
- 5 tablespoons light soy sauce
- 1 teaspoon dark soy sauce
- 3 tablespoons oil
- 5 slices ginger

Directions
1. Pat the cod fish fillets dry.
2. Season with the salt, sugar and sesame oil. Marinate for 15 min.
3. Set the Ninja Foodi to air crisp.
4. Put the fish on top of the basket. Cook at 350 degrees F for 3 min.
5. Flip and cook for 2 min. Take the fish out and set aside.
6. Put the rest of the ingredients in the pot.
7. Set it to sauté. Simmer and pour over the fish before serving.

Serving Suggestion: Sprinkle top with chopped green onion.

Nutrition value/serving: Calories 303, Total Fat 13.1g, Saturated Fat 1.9g, Cholesterol 99mg, Sodium 144mg, Total Carbohydrate 2.9g, Dietary Fiber 0.5g, Total Sugars 0.1g, Protein 41.5g, Potassium 494mg

Breathtaking Cod Fillets

Prep time: 10 min, Cooking time: 5-10 min, Serves: 4

Ingredients
- 1 pound frozen cod fish fillets
- 2 garlic cloves, halved
- 1 cup chicken broth
- 1/2 cup packed parsley
- 2 tablespoons oregano
- 2 tablespoons almonds, sliced½ teaspoon paprika

Directions
1. Take the fish out of the freezer and let it defrost
2. Take a food processor and stir in garlic, oregano, parsley, paprika, 1 tablespoon almond and process. Set your Ninja Foodi to "SAUTE" mode and add olive oil, let it heat up
3. Add remaining almonds and toast, transfer to a towel. Pour broth in a pot and add herb mixture
4. Cut fish into 4 pieces and place in a steamer basket, transfer steamer basket to the pot
5. Lock lid and cook on HIGH pressure for 3 min. Quick release pressure once has done
6. Serve steamed fish by pouring over the sauce. Enjoy!

Nutrition value/serving:
Calories: 246
Fat: 10g
Carbohydrates: 8g
Protein: 15g

Fish & Chips with Herb Sauce

Prep time: 50 min, Serves: 4

Ingredients
- 2 potatoes, sliced into strips
- Salt to taste
- 1/4 cup flour
- 1 egg
- 1 teaspoon Dijon mustard
- 3/4 cup seasoned panko bread crumbs
- 2 1/2 teaspoons olive oil
- 4 cod fish fillets

For the sauce:
- 1/4 cup light mayonnaise
- 2 tablespoons sour cream
- 2 tablespoons dill pickle, chopped
- 2 tablespoons red onion, chopped
- 1 tablespoon dill, chopped
- 1 tablespoon tarragon, chopped
- 2 teaspoons capers

Directions
1. Soak the potato strips in a bowl of water for 30 min.
2. Drain the water and pat the potatoes dry using a paper towel.
3. Place the potato strips in the Ninja Foodi basket.
4. Seal the crisping lid and choose air crisp function.
5. Cook at 360 degrees for 25 min, turning once or twice.

6. Season with the salt. Put the flour in a bowl.
7. Beat the egg and add the mustard in another bowl.
8. Mix the oil and bread crumbs on a shallow plate.
9. Coat the fish with the flour then the egg mixture, and then the oil with crumbs. Place in the basket. Cook at 360 degrees for 10 min.
10. Mix all the ingredients for the sauce and serve with the fish and fries.

Serving Suggestion: Garnish with cucumber and tomato slices.

Tip: Add cayenne pepper to make the sauce spicy.

Nutrition value/serving: Calories 409, Total Fat 12.1g, Saturated Fat 2.6g, Cholesterol 146mg, Sodium 426mg, Total Carbohydrate 27.9g, Dietary Fiber 3.2g, Total Sugars 2.6g, Protein 45.8g, Potassium 956mg

Fish Sticks

Prep time: 20 min, Serves: 2

Ingredients
- 1 lb. cod, sliced into strips
- 1/2 cup tapioca starch
- 2 eggs
- 1 teaspoon dried dill
- Salt and pepper to taste
- 1 cup almond flour
- 1 teaspoon onion powder
- 1/2 teaspoon mustard powder
- 2 tablespoons avocado oil

Directions
1. Pat the cod fillet strips dry using paper towel.
2. Place the tapioca starch in a bowl.
3. In another bowl, beat the eggs.
4. In a larger bowl, mix the dill, salt, pepper, almond flour, onion powder and mustard powder. Dip each strip in the first, second and third bowls.
5. Coat the Ninja Foodi basket with the avocado oil.
6. Place the fish strips inside. Cook at 390 degrees F for 5 min.

Serving Suggestion: Serve with tartar sauce.

Tip: You can also freeze the fish sticks and cook frozen. Just increase cooking time to 7 to 10 min.

Nutrition value/serving: Calories 549, Total Fat 15g, Saturated Fat 2.6g, Cholesterol 288mg, Sodium 246mg, Total Carbohydrate 39.4g, Dietary Fiber 2.7g, Total Sugars 2.2g, Protein 61g, Potassium 695mg

Salmon Paprika

Prep time: 5 min, Cooking time: 7 min, Serves: 4

Ingredients
- 2 wild caught salmon fillets, 1 to 1 and ½ inches thick
- 2 teaspoons avocado oil
- 2 teaspoons paprika
- Salt and pepper to taste
- Green herbs to garnish

Directions
1. Season salmon fillets with salt, pepper, paprika, and olive oil
2. Place Crisping basket in your Ninja Foodi, and pre-heat your Ninja Foodie at 390 degrees F
3. Place insert insider your Foodi and place the fillet in the insert, lock Air Crisping lid and cook for 7 min. Once done, serve the fish with herbs on top. Enjoy!

Nutrition value/serving:
Calories: 249
Fat: 11g
Carbohydrates: 1.8g
Protein: 35g

Garlic and Lemon Prawn Delight

Prep time: 5 min, Cooking time: 5 min, Serves: 4

Ingredients
- 2 tablespoons olive oil
- 1 pound prawns
- 2 tablespoons garlic, minced
- 2/3 cup fish stock
- 1 tablespoon butter
- 2 tablespoons lemon juice
- 1 tablespoon lemon zest
- Salt and pepper to taste

Directions
1. Set your Ninja Foodi to Saute mode and add butter and oil, let it heat up
2. Stir in remaining ingredients. Lock lid and cook on LOW pressure for 5 min
3. Quick release pressure. Serve and enjoy!

Nutrition value/serving: Calories: 236, Fat: 12g, Carbohydrates: 2g, Protein: 27g

Paprika Salmon

Prep time: 15 min, Serves: 2
Ingredients
- 2 salmon fillets
- 2 teaspoons avocado oil
- 2 teaspoons paprika
- Salt and pepper to taste

Directions
1. Coat the salmon with oil. Season with salt, pepper and paprika.
2. Place in the Ninja Foodi basket. Set it to air crisp function.
3. Seal the crisping lid. Cook at 390 degrees for 7 min.

Serving Suggestion: Garnish with lemon slices.
Tip: Cooking depends on the fish fillet thickness. You may need to cook longer for thicker cuts.
Nutrition value/serving: Calories 248, Total Fat 11.9g, Cholesterol 78mg, Sodium 79mg, Total Carbohydrate 1.5g, Dietary Fiber 1g, Total Sugars 0.2g, Protein 34.9g, Potassium 748mg

Kale and Salmon Delight

Prep time: 10 min, Cooking time: 5 min, Serves: 4
Ingredients
- 1 lemon, juiced
- 2 salmon fillets
- 1/4 cup extra virgin olive oil
- 1 teaspoon Dijon mustard
- 4 cups kale, thinly sliced, ribs removed
- 1 teaspoon salt
- 1 avocado, diced
- 1 cup pomegranate seeds
- 1 cup walnuts, toasted
- 1 cup goat parmesan cheese, shredded

Directions
1. Season salmon with salt and keep it on the side. Place a trivet in your Ninja Foodi
2. Place salmon over the trivet. Lock lid and cook on HIGH pressure for 15 min
3. Release pressure naturally over 10 min. Transfer salmon to a serving platter
4. Take a bowl and add kale, season with salt
5. Take another bowl and make the dressing by adding lemon juice, Dijon mustard, olive oil, and red wine vinegar. Season kale with dressing and add diced avocado, pomegranate seeds, walnuts and cheese. Toss and serve with the fish. Enjoy!

Nutrition value/serving: Calories: 234, Fat: 14g, Carbohydrates: 12g, Protein: 16g

Coconut Shrimp

Prep time: 20 min, Serves: 4
Ingredients
- 1/2 cup all purpose flour
- 1-1/2 teaspoons black pepper
- 2 eggs
- 1/3 cup panko bread crumbs
- 2/3 cup unsweetened coconut flakes
- 12 oz. shrimp, peeled and deveined
- Cooking spray
- Salt and pepper to taste
- 1/4 cup honey
- 1/4 cup lime juice

Directions
1. Mix the flour and black pepper in a bowl. In another bowl, beat the egg.
2. In the third bowl, mix the bread crumbs and coconut flakes.
3. Dip each of the shrimp in the first, second and third bowls.
4. Place in the Ninja Foodi basket. Set it to air crisp.Cover the crisping lid.
5. Cook at 400 degrees F for 8 min, turn halfway through.
6. Season with the salt and pepper.
7. Mix the remaining ingredients and serve with the shrimp.

Serving Suggestion: Garnish with fresh cilantro.
Tip: Keep the tails of the shrimp.
Nutrition value/serving: Calories 293, Total Fat 4.4g, Saturated Fat 1.3g, Cholesterol 261mg, Sodium 306mg, Total Carbohydrate 37.8g, Dietary Fiber 1.1g, Total Sugars 18.2g, Protein 25.1g, Potassium 229mg

Crispy Fish Nuggets

Prep time: 30 min, Serves: 4

Ingredients
- 1 lb. cod fillet, sliced into 8 pieces
- Salt and pepper to taste
- 1/2 cup flour
- 1 tablespoon egg with 1 teaspoon water
- 1 cup bread crumbs
- 1 tablespoon vegetable oil

Directions
1. Season the fish with salt and pepper. Cover with the flour.
2. Dip the fish in the egg wash and into the bread crumbs.
3. Place the fish nuggets in the Ninja Foodi basket. Set it to air crisp function.
4. Seal with the crisping lid. Cook at 360 degrees for 15 min.

Serving Suggestion: Serve with lemon honey tartar sauce.

Tip: Add dried dill or garlic powder to the seasoning to make it tastier.

Nutrition value/serving: Calories 234, Total Fat 5.4g, Saturated Fat 1g, Cholesterol 25mg, Sodium 229mg, Total Carbohydrate 31.4g, Dietary Fiber 1.7g, Total Sugars 1.7g, Protein 14.1g, Potassium 70mg

Adventurous Sweet and Sour Fish

Prep time: 10 min, Cooking time: 6 min, Serves: 4

Ingredients
- 2 drops liquid stevia
- 1/4 cup butter
- 1 pound fish chunks
- 1 tablespoon vinegar
- Salt and pepper to taste

Directions
1. Set your Ninja Foodi to Saute mode and add butter, let it melt
2. Add fish chunks and Saute for 3 min. Add stevia, salt, and pepper, stir
3. Lock Crisping Lid and cook on "Air Crisp" mode for 3 min at 360 degrees F
4. Serve once done and enjoy!

Nutrition value/serving: Calories: 274, Fat: 15g, Carbohydrates: 2g, Protein: 33g

Lovely Carb Soup

Prep time: 5 min, Cooking time: 6-7 hours, Serves: 4

Ingredients
- 1 cup crab meat, cubed
- 1 tablespoon garlic, minced
- Salt as needed
- Red chili flakes as needed
- 3 cups vegetable broth
- 1 teaspoon salt

Directions
1. Coat the crab cubes in lime juice and let them sit for a while
2. Add the all ingredients (including marinated crab meat) to your Ninja Foodi and lock lid
3. Cook on SLOW COOK MODE (MEDIUM) for 3 hours
4. Let it sit for a while
5. Unlock lid and set to Saute mode, simmer the soup for 5 min more on LOW
6. Stir and check to season. Enjoy!

Nutrition value/serving: Calories: 201, Fat: 11g, Carbohydrates: 12g, Protein: 13g

Heartfelt Sesame Fish

Prep time: 8 min, Cooking time: 8 min, Serves: 4

Ingredients
- 1 and 1/2 pound salmon fillet
- 1 teaspoon sesame seeds
- 1 teaspoon butter, melted
- 1/2 teaspoon salt
- 1 tablespoon apple cider vinegar
- 1/4 teaspoon rosemary, dried

Directions
1. Take apple cider vinegar and spray it to the salmon fillets
2. Then add dried rosemary, sesame seeds, butter and salt
3. Mix them well. Take butter sauce and brush the salmon properly
4. Place the salmon on the rack and lower the air fryer lid. Set the air fryer mode

5. Cook the fish for 8 min at 360 F. Serve hot and enjoy!
Nutrition value/serving: Calories: 239, Fat: 11.2g, Carbohydrates: 0.3g, Protein: 33.1g

Hot Prawns

Prep time: 15 min, Serves: 4
Ingredients
- 1 teaspoon chili flakes
- 1 teaspoon chili powder
- Salt and pepper to taste
- 12 king prawns
- 3 tablespoons mayonnaise
- 1 tablespoon ketchup
- 1 tablespoon wine vinegar

Directions
1. Combine all the spices in a bowl. Toss the prawns in the spice mixture.
2. Place the prawns in the Ninja Foodi basket. Seal the crisping lid.
3. Choose air crisp function. Cook at 360 degrees for 8 min.
4. While waiting, mix the mayo, ketchup and vinegar. Serve with the prawns.

Serving Suggestion: Place prawns in cocktails glasses.
Nutrition value/serving:
Calories 490, Total Fat 27.8g, Saturated Fat 11.4g, Cholesterol 3mg, Sodium 177mg, Total Carbohydrate 8.7g, Dietary Fiber 0.5g, Total Sugars 8.9g, Protein 0.3g, Potassium 29mg

Awesome Cherry Tomato Mackerel

Prep time: 5 min, Cooking time: 7 min, Serves: 4
Ingredients
- 4 Mackerel fillets
- 1/4 teaspoon onion powder
- 1/4 teaspoon lemon powder
- 1/4 teaspoon garlic powder
- 1/2 teaspoon salt
- 2 cups cherry tomatoes
- 3 tablespoons melted butter
- 1 and 1/2 cups of water
- 1 tablespoon black olives

Directions
1. Grease baking dish and arrange cherry tomatoes at the bottom of the dish
2. Top with fillets sprinkle all spices. Drizzle melted butter over
3. Add water to your Ninja Foodi
4. Lower rack in Ninja Foodi and place baking dish on top of the rack
5. Lock lid and cook on LOW pressure for 7 min. Quick release pressure. Serve and enjoy!
Nutrition value/serving: Calories: 325, Fat: 24g, Carbohydrates: 2g, Protein: 21g

Salt and Pepper Shrimp

Prep time: 20 min, Serves: 4
Ingredients
- 2 teaspoons peppercorns
- 1 teaspoon salt
- 1 teaspoons sugar
- 1 lb. shrimp
- 3 tablespoons rice flour
- 2 tablespoons oil

Directions
1. Set the Ninja Foodi to sauté. Roast the peppercorns for 1 minute. Let them cool.
2. Crush the peppercorns and add the salt and sugar.
3. Coat the shrimp with this mixture and then with flour.
4. Sprinkle oil on the Ninja Foodi basket. Place the shrimp on top.
5. Cook at 350 degrees for 10 min, flipping halfway through.

Serving Suggestion: Serve with fresh salad.
Tip: Add more peppercorns if you like it spicier.
Nutrition value/serving: Calories 228, Total Fat 8.9g, Saturated Fat 1.5g, Cholesterol 239mg, Sodium 859mg, Total Carbohydrate 9.3g, Dietary Fiber 0.5g, Total Sugars 1g, Protein 26.4g, Potassium 211mg

Lemon and Pepper Salmon Delight

Prep time: 5 min, Cooking time: 6 min, Serves: 4
Ingredients
- 3/4 cup of water
- Sprigs of parsley, basil, tarragon
- 1 pound salmon, skin on

- 3 teaspoons ghee
- 3/4 teaspoon salt
- 1/2 teaspoon pepper
- 1/2 lemon, sliced
- 1 red bell pepper, julienned
- 1 carrot, julienned

Directions

1. Set your Ninja Foodi to Saute mode and add water and herbs
2. Place a steamer rack and add the salmon. Drizzle ghee on top of the salmon
3. Season with pepper and salt. Cover lemon slices on top
4. Lock up the lid and cook on HIGH pressure for 3 min
5. Release the pressure naturally over 10 min
6. Transfer the salmon to a platter. Add veggies to your pot and set the pot to Saute mode
7. Cook for 1-2 min. Serve the cooked vegetables with salmon. Enjoy!

Nutrition value/serving: Calories: 464, Fat: 34g, Carbohydrates: 3g, Protein: 34g

Packets of Lemon and Dill Cod

Prep time: 10 min, Cooking time: 5-10 min, Serves: 4

Ingredients

- 2 tilapia cod fillets
- Salt, pepper and garlic powder to taste
- 2 sprigs fresh dill
- 4 slices lemon
- 2 tablespoons butter

Directions

1. Layout 2 large squares of parchment paper
2. Place fillet in center of each parchment square and season with salt, pepper and garlic powder
3. On each fillet, place 1 sprig of dill, 2 lemon slices, 1 tablespoon butter
4. Place trivet at the bottom of your Ninja Foodi. Add 1 cup water into the pot
5. Close parchment paper around fillets and fold to make a nice seal
6. Place both packets in your pot. Lock lid and cook on HIGH pressure for 5 min
7. Quick release pressure. Serve and enjoy!

Nutrition value/serving: Calories: 259, Fat: 11g, Carbohydrates: 8g, Protein: 20g

Fish Fillet with Pesto Sauce

Prep time: 20 min, Serves: 3

Ingredients

- 3 white fish fillets
- 1 tablespoon olive oil
- Salt and pepper to taste
- 2 cups fresh basil leaves
- 2 cloves garlic, crushed
- 2 tablespoons pine nuts
- 1 tablespoon Parmesan cheese, grated
- 1 cup olive oil

Directions

1. Coat the fish fillets with 1 tablespoon of olive oil. Season with the salt and pepper.
2. Place in the Ninja Foodi basket. Cook at 320 degrees for 8 min.
3. While waiting, mix the remaining ingredients in a food processor.
4. Pulse until smooth. Spread the pesto sauce on both sides of the fish before serving.

Serving Suggestion: Garnish with chopped pine nuts.

Tip: Pesto sauce can be prepared in advanced and chilled in the refrigerator for up to 3 days.

Nutrition value/serving: Calories 383, Total Fat 22.6g, Saturated Fat 4.1g, Cholesterol 125mg Sodium 188mg, Total Carbohydrate 2.2g, Dietary Fiber 0.5g, Total Sugars 0.3g, Protein 42.1g, Potassium 715mg

The Rich Guy Lobster and Butter

Prep time: 15 min, Cooking time: 20 min, Serves: 4

Ingredients

- 6 Lobster Tails
- 4 garlic cloves,
- 1/4 cup butter

Directions

1. Preheat the Ninja Foodi to 400 degrees F at first
2. Open the lobster tails gently by using kitchen scissors
3. Remove the lobster meat gently from the shells but keep it inside the shells
4. Take a plate and place it

5. Add some butter in a pan and allow it melt
6. Put some garlic cloves in it and heat it over medium-low heat
7. Pour the garlic butter mixture all over the lobster tail meat
8. Let the fryer to broil the lobster at 130 degrees F
9. Remove the lobster meat from Ninja Foodi and set aside
10. Use a fork to pull out the lobster meat from the shells entirely
11. Pour some garlic butter over it if needed. Serve and enjoy!

Nutrition value/serving: Calories: 160, Fat: 1g, Carbohydrates: 1g, Protein: 20g

Lovely Panko Cod

Prep time: 5 min, Cooking time: 15 min, Serves: 4

Ingredients
- 2 uncooked cod fillets, 6 ounces each
- 3 teaspoons kosher salt
- 3/4 cup panko bread crumbs
- 2 tablespoons butter, melted
- 1/4 cup fresh parsley, minced
- 1 lemon. Zested and juiced

Directions
1. Pre-heat your Ninja Foodi at 390 degrees F and place Air Crisper basket inside
2. Season cod and salt
3. Take a bowl and add bread crumbs, parsley, lemon juice, zest, butter, and mix well
4. Coat fillets with the bread crumbs mixture and place fillets in your Air Crisping basket
5. Lock Air Crisping lid and cook on Air Crisp mode for 15 min at 360 degrees F
6. Serve and enjoy!

Nutrition value/serving: Calories: 554, Fat: 24g, Carbohydrates: 5g, Protein: 37g

Heartfelt Air Fried Scampi

Prep time: 5 min, Cooking time: 5 min, Serves: 4

Ingredients
4 tablespoons butter
1 tablespoon lemon juice
1 tablespoon garlic, minced
2 teaspoons red pepper flakes
1 tablespoon chives, chopped
1 tablespoon basil leaves, minced
2 tablespoons chicken stock
1 pound defrosted shrimp

Directions
1. Set your Foodi to Saute mode and add butter, let the butter melt and add red pepper flakes and garlic, Saute for 2 min
2. Transfer garlic to crisping basket, add remaining ingredients (including shrimp) to the basket
3. Return basket back to the Ninja Foodi and lock the Air Crisping lid, cook for 5 min at 390 degrees F. Once done, serve with a garnish of fresh basil

Nutrition value/serving: Calories: 372, Fat: 11g, Carbohydrates: 0.9g, Protein: 63g

Buttered Up Scallops

Prep time: 10 min, Cooking time: 5 min, Serves: 4

Ingredients
- 4 garlic cloves, minced
- 4 tablespoons rosemary, chopped
- 2 pounds sea scallops
- 12 cup butter
- Salt and pepper to taste

Directions
1. Set your Ninja Foodi to Saute mode and add butter, rosemary, and garlic
2. Saute for 1 minute. Add scallops, salt, and pepper
3. Saute for 2 min. Lock Crisping lid and Crisp for 3 min at 350 degrees F. Serve and enjoy!

Nutrition value/serving:

Calories: 279

Fat: 16g

Carbohydrates: 5g

Protein: 25g

Alaskan Cod Divine

Prep time: 10 min, Cooking time: 5-10 min, Serves: 4

Ingredients
- 1 large fillet, Alaskan Cod (Frozen)
- 1 cup cherry tomatoes
- Salt and pepper to taste
- Seasoning as you need
- 2 tablespoons butter

- Olive oil as needed

Directions

1. Take an ovenproof dish small enough to fit inside your pot
2. Add tomatoes to the dish, cut large fish fillet into 2-3 serving pieces and lay them on top of tomatoes. Season with salt, pepper, and your seasoning
3. Top each fillet with 1 tablespoon butter and drizzle olive oil
4. Add 1 cup of water to the pot. Place trivet to the Ninja Foodi and place dish on the trivet
5. Lock lid and cook on HIGH pressure for 9 min. Release pressure naturally over 10 min
6. Serve and enjoy!

Nutrition value/serving: Calories: 449, Fat: 32g, Carbohydrates: 11g, Protein: 25g

Awesome Sock-Eye Salmon

Prep time: 5 min, Cooking time: 5 min, Serves: 4

Ingredients

- 4 sockeye salmon fillets
- 1 teaspoon Dijon mustard
- 1/4 teaspoon garlic, minced
- 1/4 teaspoon onion powder
- 1/4 teaspoon lemon pepper
- 1/2 teaspoon garlic powder
- 1/4 teaspoon salt
- 2 tablespoons olive oil
- 1 and 1/2 cup of water

Directions

1. Take a bowl and add mustard, lemon juice, onion powder, lemon pepper, garlic powder, salt, olive oil. Brush spice mix over salmon
2. Add water to Instant Pot. Place rack and place salmon fillets on rack
3. Lock lid and cook on LOW pressure for 7 min
4. Quick release pressure. Serve and enjoy!

Nutrition value/serving:
Calories: 353
Fat: 25g
Carbohydrates: 0.6g
Protein: 40g

Lovely Air Fried Scallops

Prep time: 5 min, Cooking time: 5 min, Serves: 4

Ingredients

- 12 scallops
- 3 tablespoons olive oil
- Salt and pepper to taste

Directions

1. Gently rub scallops with salt, pepper, and oil
2. Transfer to your Ninja Foodie's insert, and place the insert in your Foodi
3. Lock Air Crisping lid and cook for 4 min at 390 degrees F
4. Half through, make sure to give them a nice flip and keep cooking. Serve warm and enjoy!

Nutrition value/serving: Calories: 372, Fat: 11g, Carbohydrates: 0.9g, Protein: 63g

Lemon Garlic Shrimp

Prep time: 40 min, Serves: 4

Ingredients

- 1 lb. shrimp, peeled and deveined
- 1 tablespoon olive oil
- 4 cloves garlic, minced
- 1 tablespoon lemon juice
- Salt to taste

Directions

1. Mix the olive oil, salt, lemon juice and garlic. Toss shrimp in the mixture.
2. Marinate for 15 min. Place the shrimp in the Ninja Foodi basket.
3. Seal the crisping lid. Select the air crisp setting.
4. Cook at 350 degrees for 8 min. Flip and cook for 2 more min.

Serving Suggestion: Sprinkle chopped parsley on top.

Tip: Add crushed red pepper flakes if you like it spicy.

Nutrition value/serving: Calories 170, Total Fat 5.5g, Saturated Fat 1.1g, Cholesterol 239mg, Sodium 317mg, Total Carbohydrate 2.8g, Dietary Fiber 0.1g, Total Sugars 0.1g, Protein 26.1g, Potassium 209mg

Fresh Steamed Salmon

Prep time: 5 min, Cooking time: 5 min, Serves: 4

Ingredients
- 2 salmon fillets
- 1/4 cup onion, chopped
- 2 stalks green onion stalks, chopped
- 1 whole egg
- Almond meal
- Salt and pepper to taste
- 2 tablespoons olive oil

Directions
1. Add a cup of water to your Ninja Foodi and place a steamer rack on top
2. Place the fish. Season the fish with salt and pepper and lock up the lid
3. Cook on HIGH pressure for 3 min. Once done, quick release the pressure
4. Remove the fish and allow it to cool
5. Break the fillets into a bowl and add egg, yellow and green onions
6. Add 1/2 a cup of almond meal and mix with your hand. Divide the mixture into patties
7. Take a large skillet and place it over medium heat. Add oil and cook the patties. Enjoy!

Nutrition value/serving: Calories: 238, Fat: 15g, Carbohydrates: 1g, Protein: 23g

Chapter 5: Vegan and Vegetarian Recipes

Tofu, Broccoli and Carrot

Prep time: 30 min, Serves: 2

Ingredients
- 1 block tofu, sliced into cubes
- 1 tablespoon sesame oil
- 1 tablespoon soy sauce
- 3 tablespoons tapioca starch
- 2 carrots, sliced into strips
- 1 cup broccoli florets
- 2 tablespoons orange zest
- 1/2 cup orange juice
- 3 tablespoons rice vinegar
- 1 tablespoon light soy sauce
- 1 tablespoon chicken stock
- 2 tablespoons sugar
- 2 teaspoons corn starch
- 2 cloves garlic, minced
- Salt to taste

Directions
1. Coat the tofu with the sesame oil and soy sauce. Cover with tapioca starch.
2. Put the tofu cubes in the Ninja Foodi basket. Seal the crisping lid.
3. Press air crisp. Cook at 390 degrees F for 5 min. Stir the tofu and cook for another 5 min. Take the tofu out of the pot. Mix the rest of the ingredients.
4. Set the pot to sauté. Add the broccoli and carrots with the mixture.
5. Put the tofu back. Simmer for 10 min.

Serving Suggestion: Serve with a bowl of hot rice.
Tip: You can also fry the broccoli and carrots if you like them crispy.

Nutrition value/serving: Calories 296, Total Fat 9g, Saturated Fat 1.4g, Cholesterol 0mg, Sodium 616mg, Total Carbohydrate 46.4g, Dietary Fiber 4.1g, Total Sugars 21.9g, Protein 6.8g, Potassium 575mg

Smoked Chickpeas

Prep time: 30 min, Serves: 3

Ingredients
- 15 oz. chickpeas, rinsed and drained
- 1 tablespoon sunflower oil
- 2 tablespoons lemon juice
- 3/4 teaspoon smoked paprika
- 1/2 teaspoon granulated garlic
- 1/2 teaspoon ground cumin
- 1/4 teaspoon granulated onion
- Salt to taste

Directions
1. Mix all the ingredients except the oil and chickpeas. Put the chickpeas in the Ninja Foodi basket. Seal the crisping lid. Set it to air crisp function.
2. Cook at 390 degrees F for 15 min, shaking halfway through.
3. Put the chickpeas in the bowl of seasonings. Put them back to the Ninja Foodi basket.
4. Cook at 360 degrees F for 3 min.

Tip: You can also add cayenne pepper to make it spicier.

Nutrition value/serving: Calories 423, Total Fat 10.1g, Saturated Fat 1.1g, Cholesterol 0mg, Sodium 66mg, Total Carbohydrate 65.2g, Dietary Fiber 18.7g, Total Sugars 11.7g, Protein 20.8g, Potassium 957mg

Buffalo Cauliflower

Prep time: 40 min, Serves: 4

Ingredients
- 1 head cauliflower, sliced into florets.
- 1 cup almond flour
- 1 teaspoon vegan bouillon granules
- 1/4 teaspoon paprika
- 1/4 teaspoon chili powder
- 1/4 teaspoon cayenne pepper
- 1/4 teaspoon dried chipotle chili flakes
- 1 cup soy milk
- Cooking spray
- 2 tablespoons vegan butter
- 1/2 cup hot sauce
- 2 cloves garlic, minced

Directions
1. Mix the almond flour, vegan bouillon granules, paprika, chili powder, cayenne pepper, and dried

chipotle chile flakes. Gradually add the milk. Mix well.
2. Toss the cauliflower in the mixture. Spray the Ninja Foodi basket with oil.
3. Put the cauliflower on the basket. Cook at 390 degrees F for 20 min.
4. Turn the cauliflower halfway through. Take the cauliflower out of the pot. Set aside.
5. Set the pot to sauté. Heat the butter, garlic and hot sauce. Simmer for 5 min.
6. Pour over the cauliflower florets.
Serving Suggestion: Garnish with freshly parsley.
Tip: You can also use almond or hemp milk.
Nutrition value/serving: Calories 199, Total Fat 9.6g, Saturated Fat 0.9g, Cholesterol 0mg, Sodium 1634mg, Total Carbohydrate 20.2g, Dietary Fiber 6.1g, Total Sugars 8.9g, Protein 10.2g, Potassium 658mg

Garlic Pepper Potato Chips

Prep time: 20 min, Serves: 2
Ingredients
- 1 large potato, sliced into thin chips
- Cooking spray
- Salt and garlic powder to taste
- 1 teaspoon black pepper

Directions
1. Spray oil on the Ninja Foodi basket.
2. Season the potato with the salt, garlic powder and black pepper.
3. Place potato chips on the basket. Seal the crisping lid. Set it to air crisp.
4. Cook at 450 degrees F for 10 min or until golden and crispy.
Serving Suggestion: Serve with mayo dip.
Tip: Press moisture out of the potatoes using paper towel.
Nutrition value/serving: Calories 147, Total Fat 0.5g, Saturated Fat 0.1g, Cholesterol 0mg, Sodium 12mg, Total Carbohydrate 32.9g, Dietary Fiber 4.3g, Total Sugars 1.5g, Protein 3.8g, Potassium 790mg

Crispy Tofu

Prep time: 1 hour, Serves: 4
Ingredients
- 1 teaspoon seasoned rice vinegar
- 2 tablespoons low sodium soy sauce
- 2 teaspoons toasted sesame oil
- 1 block firm tofu, sliced into cubes
- 1 tablespoon potato starch
- Cooking spray

Directions
1. In a bowl, mix the vinegar, soy sauce, and sesame oil.
2. Marinate the tofu for 30 min. Coat the tofu with potato starch.
3. Spray the Ninja Foodi basket with oil. Seal the crisping lid. Choose the air crisp setting. Cook at 370 degrees for 20 min, flipping halfway through.
Serving Suggestion: Serve with soy sauce and vinegar dipping sauce.
Tip: Press the tofu dry using paper towel.
Nutrition value/serving: Calories 137, Total Fat 3.4g, Saturated Fat 0.5g, Cholesterol 0mg, Sodium 310mg, Total Carbohydrate 24g, Dietary Fiber 0.5g, Total Sugars 0.4g, Protein 2.3g, Potassium 50mg

Crazy Fresh Onion Soup

Prep time: 5 min, Cooking time: 10-15 min, Serves: 4
Ingredients
- 2 tablespoons avocado oil
- 8 cups yellow onion
- 1 tablespoon balsamic vinegar
- 6 cups of pork stock
- 1 teaspoon salt
- 2 bay leaves
- 2 large sprigs, fresh thyme

Directions
1. Cut up the onion in half through the root
2. Peel them and slice into thin half moons
3. Set the pot to Saute mode and add oil, one the oil is hot and add onions
4. Cook for about 15 min
5. Add balsamic vinegar and scrape any fond from the bottom
6. Add stock, bay leaves, salt, and thyme
7. Lock up the lid and cook on HIGH pressure for 10 min
8. Release the pressure naturally
9. Discard the bay leaf and thyme stems

10. Blend the soup using an immersion blender and serve!
Nutrition value/serving: Calories: 454, Fat: 31g, Carbohydrates: 7g, Protein: 27g

Fried Tempeh

Prep time: 40 min, Serves: 4
Ingredients
- 200g tempeh, sliced into chunks
- 2 tablespoons vegan mayonnaise
- 3 tablespoons bread crumbs

Sauce:
- 2 tablespoons Korean red pepper paste
- 2 cloves garlic, crushed
- 1 tablespoon maple syrup
- 1 tablespoon soy sauce
- 1 tablespoon water
- Salt and pepper to taste

Directions
1. Put the mayo in one bowl and the bread crumbs in another. Dilute the mayo with water. Coat each tempeh with mayo and then with the bread crumbs.
2. Place in the Ninja Foodi basket. Seal the crisping lid. Set it to air crisp.
3. Cook at 350 degrees F for 15 min or until golden and crispy.
4. Stir every 5 min. Take them out and set aside.
5. Mix all the sauce ingredients. Put in the pot. Set it to sauté. Simmer for 5 min. Add the tempeh to the sauce and toss to coat evenly.

Serving Suggestion: Top with sesame seeds.
Tip: Cook in batches for even browning.
Nutrition value/serving: Calories 131, Total Fat 7.2g, Saturated Fat 1.1g, Cholesterol 0mg, Sodium 286mg, Total Carbohydrate 9.4g, Dietary Fiber 0.1g, Total Sugars 3.1g, Protein 9.6g, Potassium 231mg

Garlic Chips

Prep time: 1 hour, Serves: 2
Ingredients
- 2 potatoes, sliced into chips
- Salt to taste
- 4 cloves garlic, minced
- 2 tablespoons vegan parmesan

Directions
1. Put the potatoes in a bowl of water. Stir in the salt. Soak for 20 to 30 min.
2. Drain the potatoes and pat try. Season with the garlic and vegan parmesan.
3. Arrange the chips on the Ninja Foodi basket. Seal the crisping lid.
4. Set it to air crisp function. Cook at 350 degrees for 10 min or until crispy.
5. Flip every 3 to 5 min.

Serving Suggestion: Serve with hot sauce or mayo.
Tip: Do not overcrowd to cook evenly.
Nutrition value/serving: Calories 156, Total Fat 0.2g, Saturated Fat 0.1g, Cholesterol 0mg, Sodium 91mg, Total Carbohydrate 35.4g, Dietary Fiber 5.2g, Total Sugars 2.5g, Protein 4g, Potassium 891mg

Delicious Beet Borscht

Prep time: 5 min, Cooking time: 45 min, Serves: 6
Ingredients
- 8 cups beets
- 1/2 cup celery, diced
- 1/2 cup carrots, diced
- 2 garlic cloves, diced
- 1 medium onion, diced
- 3 cups cabbage, shredded
- 6 cups beef stock
- 1 bay leaf
- 1 tablespoon salt
- 1/2 tablespoon thyme
- 1/4 cup fresh dill, chopped
- 1/2 cup of coconut yogurt

Directions
1. Add the washed beets to a steamer in the Ninja Foodi
2. Add 1 cup of water. Steam for 7 min
3. Perform a quick release and drop into an ice bath
4. Carefully peel off the skin and dice the beets
5. Transfer the diced beets, celery, carrots, onion, garlic, cabbage, stock, bay leaf, thyme and salt to your Instant Pot. Lock up the lid and set the pot to SOUP mode, cook for 45 min
6. Release the pressure naturally. Transfer to bowls and top with a dollop of dairy-free yogurt
7. Enjoy with a garnish of fresh dill!

Nutrition value/serving: Calories: 625, Fats: 46g, Carbs:19g, Protein:90g

Cauliflower Stir Fry

Prep time: 30 min, Serves: 4

Ingredients
- 1 head cauliflower, sliced into florets
- 3/4 cup white onion, sliced
- 5 cloves garlic, minced
- 1-1/2 tablespoons tamari
- 1 tablespoon rice vinegar
- 1/2 teaspoon coconut sugar
- 1 tablespoon hot sauce

Directions
1. Put the cauliflower in the Ninja Foodi basket. Seal the crisping lid.
2. Select the air crisp setting. Cook at 350 degrees F for 10 min.
3. Add the onion, stir and cook for additional 10 min.
4. Add the garlic, and cook for 5 min. Mix the rest of the ingredients.
5. Pour over the cauliflower before serving.

Serving Suggestion: Garnish with chopped scallions.

Nutrition value/serving: Calories 93, Total Fat 3g, Sodium 510mg, Total Carbohydrates 12g, Dietary Fiber 3g, Sugars 4g, Protein 4g, Potassium 519mg

Feisty Maple Dredged Carrots

Prep time: 10 min, Cooking time: 4 min, Serves: 4

Ingredients
- 2-pound carrot
- 1/4 cup raisins
- Pepper as needed
- 1 cup of water
- 1 tablespoon butter
- 1 tablespoon sugar-free Keto friendly maple syrup

Directions
1. Wash, peel the skin and slice the carrots diagonally
2. Add the carrots, raisins, water to your Ninja Foodi
3. Lock up the lid and cook on HIGH pressure for 4 min. Perform a quick release
4. Strain the carrots. Add butter and maple syrup to the warm Ninja Foodi and mix well
5. Transfer the strained carrots back to the pot and stir to coat with maple sauce and butter
6. Serve with a bit of pepper. Enjoy!

Nutrition value/serving: Calories: 358, Fats: 12g, Carbs: 20g, Protein: 1g

Onion Rings

Prep time: 30 min, Serves: 4

Ingredients
- 3 yellow onions, sliced into rings
- 1/2 cup almond flour
- 2/3 cup unsweetened coconut milk
- 1/2 teaspoon paprika
- 1/4 teaspoon turmeric
- Salt to taste

Directions
1. Mix all the ingredients except the onion rings in a large bowl.
2. Coat each onion ring with the mixture. Place in the Ninja Foodi basket.
3. Seal the crisping lid. Set it to air crisp.
4. Cook at 400 degrees for 10 min, flipping halfway through.

Serving Suggestion: Serve with ketchup or hot sauce.

Tip: This is best served warm.

Nutrition value/serving: Calories 147, Total Fat 11.3g, Saturated Fat 8.6g, Cholesterol 0mg, Sodium 49mg, Total Carbohydrate 10.9g, Dietary Fiber 3.2g, Total Sugars 4.9g, Protein 2.6g, Potassium 235mg

Elegant Zero Crust Kale and Mushroom Quiche

Prep time: 5 min, Cooking time: 9 hours, Serves: 4

Ingredients
- 6 large eggs
- 2 tablespoons unsweetened almond milk
- 2 ounces low –fat feta cheese, crumbled
- 1/4 cup parmesan cheese, grated
- 1 and 1/2 teaspoons Italian seasoning
- 4 ounces mushrooms, sliced
- 2 cups kale, chopped

Directions
1. Grease the inner pot of your Ninja Foodi
2. Take a large bowl and whisk in eggs, cheese, almond milk, seasoning and mix it well
3. Stir in kale and mushrooms. Pour the mix into Ninja Foodi. Gently stir
4. Place lid and cook on SLOW COOK Mode(LOW) for 8-9 hours. Serve and enjoy!

Nutrition value/serving: Calories: 112, Fat: 7g, Carbohydrates: 4g, Protein: 10g

Vegan Cheese Sticks

Prep time: 8 hours and 30 min, Serves: 3-4
Ingredients
- 1 block vegan mozzarella, sliced into strips
- 1 bag vegan chips
- 1-1/2 cups almond flour
- 2 cups vegan milk
- 1/4 cup nutritional yeast

Directions
1. Put the chips and nutritional yeast in the food processor. Pulse until powdery.
2. Dip each cheese strip in the milk and cover with flour.
3. Dip into the milk again and coat with the powdered chips.
4. Place in the freezer for 8 hours. Add the frozen cheese sticks to the Ninja Foodi basket. Seal the crisping lid. Set it to air crisp. Cook at 380 degrees for 10 min.

Serving Suggestion: Serve with vegetable sticks.
Nutrition value/serving: Calories 116, Total Fat 4.1g, Saturated Fat 2.1g, Cholesterol 8mg, Sodium 87mg, Total Carbohydrate 9.7g, Dietary Fiber 5g, Total Sugars 0g, Protein 12.7g, Potassium 480mg

Slow-Cooked Brussels

Prep time: 5 min, Cooking time: 4 hours, Serves: 4
Ingredients
- 1 pound Brussels sprouts, bottom trimmed and cut
- 1 tablespoon olive oil
- 1 -1/2 tablespoon Dijon mustard
- 1/4 cup of water
- Salt and pepper as needed
- 1/2 teaspoon dried tarragon

Directions
1. Add Brussels, salt, water, pepper, mustard to Ninja Foodi
2. Add dried tarragon and stir
3. Lock lid and cook on SLOW COOK MODE (LOW) for 5 hours until the Brussels are tender
4. Stir well and add Dijon over Brussels. Stir and enjoy!

Nutrition value/serving: Calories: 83, Fat: 4g, Carbohydrates: 11g, Protein: 4g

Fried Soy Curls

Prep time: 30 min, Serves: 2
Ingredients
- 4 oz. soy curls
- 3 cups hot water
- 1/4 cup fine ground cornmeal
- 1/4 cup nutritional yeast
- 1 teaspoon poultry seasoning
- 1 teaspoons Cajun seasoning
- Salt and pepper to taste

Directions
1. Soak the soy curls in hot water for 10 min. Drain in a strainer.
2. Press the water out. In a bowl, mix the rest of the ingredients.
3. Coat each soy curl with the breading. Place in the Ninja Foodi basket.
4. Seal the crisping lid. Set it to air crisp function.
5. Cook at 380 degrees for 5 min. Season with the salt and pepper.

Serving Suggestion: Serve with mashed potatoes and gravy.
Nutrition value/serving: Calories100, Total Fat 1g, Saturated Fat 19g, Fiber 3g, Carbohydrates 17g, Protein 4g, Cholesterol 22mg, Sugars 2g, Sodium 19mg, Potassium 174mg

The Creative Mushroom Stroganoff

Prep time: 5 min, Cooking time: 10 min, Serves: 6
Ingredients
- 1/4 cup unsalted butter, cubed
- 1 pound cremini mushrooms, halved
- 1 large onion, halved
- 4 garlic cloves, minced
- 2 cups vegetable broth

- 1/2 teaspoon salt
- 1/4 teaspoon fresh black pepper
- 1 and 1/2 cups sour cream
- 1/4 cup fresh flat-leaf parsley, chopped
- 1 cup grated parmesan cheese

Directions

1. Add butter, mushrooms, onion, garlic, vegetable broth, salt, pepper, and paprika
2. Gently stir and lock lid. Cook on HIGH pressure for 5 min
3. Release pressure naturally over 10 min
4. Serve by stirring in sour cream and with a garnish of parsley and parmesan cheese. Enjoy!

Nutrition value/serving: Calories: 453, Fat: 37g, Carbohydrates: 11g, Protein: 19g

Very Rich and Creamy Asparagus Soup

Prep time: 10 min, Cooking time: 5-10 min, Serves: 4

Ingredients

- 1 tablespoon olive oil
- 3 green onions, sliced crosswise into ¼ inch pieces
- 1 pound asparagus, tough ends removed, cut into 1 inch pieces
- 4 cups vegetable stock
- 1 tablespoon unsalted butter
- 1 tablespoon almond flour
- 2 teaspoon salt
- 1 teaspoon white pepper
- 1/2 cup heavy cream

Directions

1. Set your Ninja Foodi to "Saute" mode and add oil, let it heat up
2. Add green onions and Saute for a few min, add asparagus and stock
3. Lock lid and cook on HIGH pressure for 5 min
4. Take a small saucepan and place it over low heat, add butter, flour and stir until the mixture foams and turns into a golden beige, this is your blond roux
5. Remove from heat. Release pressure naturally over 10 min
6. Open the lid and add roux, salt, and pepper to the soup
7. Use an immersion blender to puree the soup
8. Taste and season accordingly, swirl in cream and enjoy!

Nutrition value/serving: Calories: 192, Fat: 14g, Carbohydrates: 8g, Protein: 6g

Garlic and Ginger Red Cabbage Platter

Prep time: 10 min, Cooking time: 8 min, Serves: 4

Ingredients

- 2 tablespoon coconut oil
- 1 tablespoon butter
- 3 garlic cloves, crushed
- 2 teaspoon fresh ginger, grated
- 8 cups red cabbage, shredded
- 1 teaspoon salt
- 1/2 a teaspoon pepper
- 1/3 cup water

Directions

1. Set your Ninja Foodi to Saute mode and add coconut oil and butter, allow to heat up
2. Add garlic and ginger and mix. Add cabbage, pepper, salt, and water
3. Mix well and lock up the lid, cook on HIGH pressure for 5 min
4. Perform a quick release and mix. Serve and enjoy!

Nutrition value/serving: Calories: 96, Fat: 6g, Carbohydrates: 9g, Protein: 1.8g

Cheddar Cauliflower Bowl

Prep time: 10 min, Cooking time: 5 min, Serves: 8

Ingredients

- 1/4 cup butter
- 1/2 sweet onion, chopped
- 1 head cauliflower, chopped
- 4 cups herbed vegetable stock
- 1/2 teaspoon ground nutmeg
- 1 cup heavy whip cream
- Salt and pepper as needed
- 1 cup cheddar cheese, shredded

Directions

1. Set your Ninja Foodi to sauté mode and add butter, let it heat up and melt
2. Add onion and Cauliflower, Saute for 10 min until tender and lightly browned
3. Add vegetable stock and nutmeg, bring to a boil

4. Lock lid and cook on HIGH pressure for 5 min, quick release pressure once done
5. Remove pot and from Foodi and stir in heavy cream, puree using an immersion blender
6. Season with more salt and pepper and serve with a topping of cheddar. Enjoy!

Nutrition value/serving: Calories: 227, Fat: 21g, Carbohydrates: 4g, Protein: 8g

Potato Wedges

Prep time: 30 min, Serves: 4

Ingredients
- 1 lb. potatoes, sliced into wedges
- 1 teaspoon olive oil
- Salt and pepper to taste
- 1/2 teaspoon garlic powder

Directions
1. Coat the potatoes with oil. Season with the salt, pepper and garlic powder.
2. Add the potatoes in the Ninja Foodi basket. Cover with the crisping lid.
3. Set it to air crisp. Cook at 400 degrees F for 16 min, flipping halfway through.

Serving Suggestion: Serve with vegan cheese sauce.

Tip: Soak the potatoes in water then pat dry with paper towel.

Nutrition value/serving: Calories 179, Total Fat 2.6g, Saturated Fat 0.4g, Cholesterol 0mg, Sodium 14mg, Total Carbohydrate 36.2g, Dietary Fiber 5.5g, Total Sugars 2.8g, Protein 3.9g, Potassium 931mg

The Original Sicilian Cauliflower Roast

Prep time: 10 min, Cooking time: 10 min, Serves: 4

Ingredients
- 1 medium cauliflower head, leaves removed
- 1/4 cup olive oil
- 1 teaspoon red pepper, crushed
- 1/2 cup of water
- 2 tablespoons capers, rinsed and minced
- 1/2 cup parmesan cheese, grated
- 1 tablespoon fresh parsley, chopped

Directions
1. Take the Ninja Foodi and start by adding water and place the cook and crisp basket inside the pot. Cut an "X" on the head of cauliflower by using a knife and slice it about halfway down
2. Take a basket and transfer the cauliflower in it
3. Then put on the pressure lid and seal it and set it on low pressure for 3 min
4. Add olive oil, capers, garlic, and crushed red pepper into it and mix them well
5. Once the cauliflower is cooked, do a quick release and remove the lid
6. Pour in the oil and spice mixture on the cauliflower
7. Spread equally on the surface then sprinkle some Parmesan cheese from the top
8. Close the pot with crisping lid. Set it on Air Crisp mode to 390 degrees F for 10 min
9. Once done, remove the cauliflower flower the Ninja Foodi transfer it into a serving plate
10. Cut it up into pieces and transfer them to serving plates. Sprinkle fresh parsley from the top
11. Serve and enjoy!

Nutrition value/serving: Calories: 119, Fat: 10g, Carbohydrates: 5g, Protein: 2.2g

Slowly Cooked Lemon Artichokes

Prep time: 10 min, Cooking time: 5 hours, Serves: 4

Ingredients
- 5 large artichokes
- 1 teaspoon of sea salt
- 2 stalks celery, sliced
- 2 large carrots, cut into matchsticks
- Juice from 1/2 a lemon
- 1/4 teaspoon black pepper
- 1 teaspoon dried thyme
- 1 tablespoon dried rosemary
- Lemon wedges for garnish

Directions
1. Remove the stalk from your artichokes and remove the tough outer shell
2. Transfer the chokes to your Ninja Foodi and add 2 cups of boiling water
3. Add celery, lemon juice, salt, carrots, black pepper, thyme, rosemary
4. Cook on Slow Cook mode (HIGH) for 4-5 hours

5. Serve the artichokes with lemon wedges. Serve and enjoy!

Nutrition value/serving: Calories: 205, Fat: 2g, Carbohydrates: 12g, Protein: 34g

The Authentic Zucchini Pesto Meal

Prep time: 10 min, Cooking time: 10 min, Serves: 4

Ingredients
- 1 tablespoon olive oil
- 1 onion, chopped
- 2 and 1/2 pound roughly chopped zucchini
- 1/2 cup of water
- 1 and 1/2 teaspoon salt
- 1 bunch basil leaves
- 2 garlic cloves, minced
- 1 tablespoon extra-virgin olive oil
- Zucchini for making zoodles

Direction
1. Set the Ninja Foodi to Saute mode and add olive oil
2. Once the oil is hot, add onion and Saute for 4 min
3. Add zucchini, water, and salt. Lock up the lid and cook on HIGH pressure for 3 min
4. Release the pressure naturally. Add basil, garlic, and leaves
5. Use an immersion blender to blend everything well until you have a sauce-like consistency
6. Take the extra zucchini and pass them through a Spiralizer to get noodle like shapes
7. Toss the Zoodles with sauce and enjoy!

Nutrition value/serving: Calories: 71, Fat: 4g, Carbohydrates: 6g, Protein: 3g

Supreme Cauliflower Soup

Prep time: 10 min, Cooking time: 5 min, Serves: 4

Ingredients
- 1/2 a small onion, chopped
- 2 tablespoons butter
- 1 large head of cauliflower, leaves and stems removed, coarsely chopped
- 2 cups chicken stock
- 1 teaspoon garlic powder
- 1 teaspoon salt
- 4 ounces cream cheese, cut into cubes
- 1 cup sharp cheddar cheese, cut
- 1/2 cup cream
- Extra cheddar, sour cream bacon strips, green onion for topping

Directions
1. Peel the onion and chop up into small pieces
2. Cut the leaves of the cauliflower and steam, making sure to keep the core intact
3. Coarsely chop the cauliflower into pieces
4. Set your Ninja Foodi to Saute mode and add onion, cook for 2-3 min
5. Add chopped cauliflower, stock, salt, and garlic powder
6. Lock up the lid and cook on HIGH pressure for 5 min. Perform a quick release
7. Prepare the toppings. Use an immersion blender to puree your soup in the Ninja Foodi
8. Serve your soup with a topping of sliced green onions, cheddar, crumbled bacon. Enjoy!

Nutrition value/serving: Calories: 438, Fat: 36g, Carbohydrates: 8g, Protein: 22g

Fried Broccoli

Prep time: 15 min, Serves: 2

Ingredients
- 4 cups broccoli florets
- 2 tablespoons coconut oil
- 1 tablespoon nutritional yeast
- Salt and pepper to taste

Directions
1. Combine all the ingredients in a bowl. Place the broccoli in the Ninja Foodi basket.
2. Seal the crisping lid. Choose air crisp setting. Cook at 370 degrees F for 5 min.

Serving Suggestion: Serve as side dish to main course.

Tip: Cook on a single layer to cook evenly.

Nutrition value/serving: Calories 197, Total Fat 14.5g, Saturated Fat 11.8g, Cholesterol 0mg, Sodium 63mg, Total Carbohydrate 14.4g, Dietary Fiber 6g, Total Sugars 3.1g, Protein 7.4g, Potassium 697mg

Brussels Sprouts

Prep time: 20 min, Serves: 4

Ingredients
- 1 lb. Brussels sprouts

- 2 teaspoons olive oil
- 1/4 teaspoon garlic powder
- 1/4 teaspoon salt

Directions

1. Put the Brussels sprouts in a bowl. Pour the olive oil into the bowl.
2. Season the sprouts with garlic powder and salt. Put the sprouts on the basket.
3. Seal the crisping lid. Set it to air crisp function.
4. Cook at 370 degrees F for 6 min, flipping halfway through.

Serving Suggestion: Serve as side dish to a main course.

Tip: Trim the brown leaves of the Brussels sprouts.

Nutrition value/serving: Calories 139, Total Fat 5.4g, Saturated Fat 0.9g, Cholesterol 0mg, Sodium 347mg, Total Carbohydrate 20.9g, Dietary Fiber 8.5g, Total Sugars 5g, Protein 7.8g, Potassium 885mg

A Prosciutto and Thyme Eggs

Prep time: 10 min, Cooking time: 5 min, Serves: 4

Ingredients

- 4 kale leaves
- 4 prosciutto slices
- 3 tablespoons heavy cream
- 4 hardboiled eggs
- 1/4 teaspoon pepper
- 1/4 teaspoon salt
- 1 and 1/2 cups of water

Directions

1. Peel eggs and wrap in kale. Wrap in prosciutto and sprinkle salt and pepper
2. Add water to your Ninja Foodi and lower trivet. Place eggs inside and lock lid
3. Cook on HIGH pressure for 5 min. Quick release pressure. Serve and enjoy!

Nutrition value/serving: Calories: 290, Fat: 23g, Carbohydrates: 4g, Protein: 16g

Vegetable Fritters

Prep time: 30 min, Serves: 6

Ingredients

- 3 tablespoons ground flaxseed mixed with 1/2 cup water
- 2 potatoes, shredded
- 2 cups frozen mixed vegetables
- 1 cup frozen peas, thawed
- 1/2 cup onion, chopped
- 1/4 cup fresh cilantro, chopped
- 1/2 cup almond flour
- Salt to taste
- Cooking spray

Directions

1. Combine all the ingredients in a bowl. Form patties. Spray each patty with oil.
2. Transfer to the Ninja Foodi basket. Set it to air crisp. Close the crisping lid.
3. Cook at 360 degrees F for 15 min, flipping halfway through.

Tip: You can also omit the cooking spray for an oil-free recipe.

Nutrition value/serving: Calories 171, Total Fat 0.5g, Saturated Fat 0.1g, Cholesterol 0mg, Sodium 107mg, Total Carbohydrate 35.7g, Dietary Fiber 9.1g, Total Sugars 6.5g, Iron 2mg

The Veggie Lover's Onion and Tofu Platter

Prep time: 8 min, Cooking time: 12 min, Serves: 4

Ingredients

- 4 tablespoons butter
- 2 tofu blocks, pressed and cubed into 1-inch pieces
- Salt and pepper to taste
- 1 cup cheddar cheese, grated
- 2 medium onions, sliced

Directions

1. Take a bowl and add tofu, season with salt and pepper
2. Set your Foodi to Saute mode and add butter, let it melt
3. Add onions and Saute for 3 min. Add seasoned tofu and cook for 2 min more
4. Add cheddar and gently stir
5. Lock the lid and bring down the Air Crisp mode, let the dish cook on "Air Crisp" mode for 3 min at 340 degrees F. Once done, take the dish out, serve and enjoy!

Nutrition value/serving: Calories: 184, Fat: 12g, Carbohydrates: 5g, Protein: 12g

Pepper Jack Cauliflower Meal

Prep time: 5 min, Cooking time: 3 hours 35 min, Serves: 6

Ingredients
- 1 head cauliflower
- 1/4 cup whipping cream
- 4 ounces cream cheese
- 1/2 teaspoon pepper
- 1 teaspoon salt
- 2 tablespoons butter
- 4 ounces pepper jack cheese
- 6 bacon slices, crumbled

Directions
1. Grease Ninja Foodi and add listed ingredients (except cheese and bacon)
2. Stir and Lock lid, cook SLOW COOK MODE (LOW) for 3 hours
3. Remove lid and add cheese, stir. Lock lid again and cook for 1 hour more
4. Garnish with bacon crumbles and enjoy!

Nutrition value/serving:
Calories: 272
Fat: 21g
Carbohydrates: 5g
Protein: 10g

Well Dressed Brussels

Prep time: 10 min, Cooking time: 4-5 hours, Serves: 4

Ingredients
- 2 pounds Brussels, halved
- 2 red onions, sliced
- 2 tablespoons apple cider vinegar
- 1 tablespoon extra-virgin olive oil
- 1 teaspoon ground cinnamon
- 1/2 cup pecans, chopped

Directions
1. Add Brussels and onions to Ninja Foodi. Take a small bowl and add cinnamon, vinegar, olive oil
2. Pour mixture over sprouts and toss
3. Place lid and cook on SLOW COOK MODE (LOW) for 4-5 hours. Enjoy!

Nutrition value/serving: Calories: 176, Fat: 10g, Carbohydrates: 14g, Protein: 4g

Summertime Vegetable Platter

Prep time: 5 min, Cooking time: 3 hours 5 min, Serves: 6

Ingredients
- 1 cup grape tomatoes
- 2 cups okra
- 1 cup mushrooms
- 2 cups yellow bell peppers
- 1 and 1/2 cup red onions
- 2 and 1/2 cups zucchini
- 1/2 cup olive oil
- 1/2 cup balsamic vinegar
- 1 tablespoon fresh thyme, chopped
- 2 tablespoons fresh basil, chopped

Directions
1. Slice and chop okra, onions, tomatoes, zucchini, mushrooms
2. Add veggies to a large container and mix
3. Take another dish and add oil and vinegar, mix in thyme and basil
4. Toss the veggies into Ninja Foodi and pour marinade. Stir well
5. Close lid and cook on 3 hours on SLOW COOK MOD (HIGH), making sure to stir after every hour

Nutrition value/serving: Calories: 233, Fat: 18g, Carbohydrates: 14g, Protein: 3g

Chapter 6: Soups and Stews Recipes

Chicken & Lemon Soup

Prep time: 30 min, Serves: 8

Ingredients
- 1 tablespoon olive oil
- 1 onion, diced
- 2 carrots, sliced
- 1 stalk celery, diced
- Salt and pepper to taste
- 2 chicken breasts, sliced into cubes
- 6 cups chicken broth
- 2 tablespoons butter
- 2 tablespoons flour dissolved in 2 tablespoons water
- 1/4 cup lemon juice

Directions
1. Set the Ninja Foodi to sauté.
2. Pour in the olive oil.
3. Add the onion and cook for 3 min.
4. Add the carrots, celery, salt and pepper.
5. Cook for 5 min.
6. Add the chicken and cook until brown on all sides.
7. Pour in the broth.
8. Seal the pot.
9. Set it to pressure.
10. Cook at high pressure for 5 min.
11. Release the pressure naturally.
12. Stir in the butter, flour and water mixture, and lemon juice.
13. Simmer for 5 min.

Serving Suggestion: Top with feta cheese cubes.
Tip: Use freshly squeezed lemon juice.

Nutrition value/serving:
Calories 200, Total Fat 11.1g, Saturated Fat 4.2g, Cholesterol 52mg, Sodium 850mg, Total Carbohydrate 4.9g, Dietary Fiber 1g, Total Sugars 2.7g, Protein 18.9g, Potassium 433mg

Cauliflower Soup

Prep time: 20 min, Serves: 4

Ingredients
- 2 tablespoons olive oil
- 1 onion, chopped
- 8 cups cauliflower florets
- 3 cups chicken stock
- 1 teaspoon garlic powder
- Salt to taste
- 4 oz. cream cheese, sliced into cubes
- 1 cup cheddar cheese, shredded
- 1/2 cup cream

Directions
1. Choose sauté in the Ninja Foodi.
2. Add the olive oil and cook onion for 2 min.
3. Add the rest of the ingredients except the cheeses and cream.
4. Set the pot to pressure.
5. Cover the pot.
6. Cook at high pressure for 5 min.
7. Release the pressure quickly.
8. Transfer the cauliflower in a food processor.
9. Pulse until smooth.
10. Put it back to the pot.
11. Stir in the cheeses and cream.
12. Serving Suggestion: Top with sour cream and crispy bacon bits.

Tip: Simmer to thicken the soup.

Nutrition value/serving: Calories 363, Total Fat 28.6g, Saturated Fat 14.4g, Cholesterol 67mg, Sodium 942mg, Total Carbohydrate 16.3g, Dietary Fiber 5.7g, Total Sugars 7.5g, Protein 14.3g, Potassium 737mg

Beef & Vegetable Soup

Prep time: 1 hour and 10 min, Serves: 6

Ingredients
- 2 tablespoons olive oil
- 2 lb. stew beef
- 2 teaspoons all purpose seasoning
- 8 oz. tomato sauce
- 23 oz. tomato soup
- 1 tablespoon garlic powder
- 1 tablespoon onion powder
- Salt and pepper to taste
- 14 oz. green beans
- 14 oz. carrots, sliced

- 15 oz. sweet corn
- 1 cup potatoes, diced
- 1 cup water
- 2 cups beef broth

Directions
1. Hit the sauté button in the Ninja Foodi.
2. Add the oil and beef.
3. Sprinkle seasoning and toss to coat the beef evenly.
4. Cook until brown on all sides.
5. Drain the liquid.
6. In a bowl, mix the tomato sauce, tomato soup, garlic powder, onion powder, salt and pepper.
7. Pour this into the pot.
8. Add the rest of the ingredients.
9. Mix well.
10. Cover the pot.
11. Set it to pressure.
12. Cook at high pressure for 35 min.
13. Release the pressure naturally.

Nutrition value/serving: Calories 564, Total Fat 14.6g, Saturated Fat 1.3g, Cholesterol 0mg, Sodium 871mg, Total Carbohydrate 79.9g, Dietary Fiber 12.8g, Total Sugars 21.3g, Protein 39.1g, Potassium 1471mg

Beef & Potato Stew

Prep time: 1 hour and 15 min, Serves: 6

Ingredients
- 2 lb. boneless beef, sliced into cubes
- Salt and pepper to taste
- 3 tablespoons all-purpose flour
- 3 tablespoons olive oil
- 1 onion, chopped
- 1/2 teaspoon fresh rosemary leaves, chopped
- 1/2 teaspoon fresh thyme leaves, chopped
- 1/4 teaspoon dried oregano
- 1 tablespoon balsamic vinegar
- 2 cups beef broth
- 3 potatoes, sliced into cubes
- 1/2 teaspoon Worcestershire sauce

Directions
1. Season the beef with salt and pepper.
2. Coat with flour.
3. Pour the oil into the Ninja Foodi.
4. Press sauté.
5. Add the onion and cook for 1 minute.
6. Add the beef and cook until brown on both sides.
7. Add the rest of the ingredients.
8. Cover the pot.
9. Set it to pressure.
10. Cook at high pressure for 30 min.
11. Release pressure naturally.

Serving Suggestion: Garnish with chopped fresh parsley.

Tip: This can be stored in the refrigerator for up to 4 days.

Nutrition value/serving: Calories 433, Total Fat 16.5g, Saturated Fat 4.5g, Cholesterol 127mg, Sodium 360mg, Total Carbohydrate 22g, Dietary Fiber 3.2g, Total Sugars 2.3g, Protein 47.1g, Potassium 1109mg

Potato Soup

Prep time: 1 hour and 15 min, Serves: 12

Ingredients
- 3 tablespoons butter
- 2 cloves garlic, minced
- 6 potatoes, diced
- 1/2 teaspoon pepper
- 2 teaspoons onion powder
- 1 cup chicken broth
- 1/4 teaspoon salt
- 2 cups milk
- 4 oz. cream cheese, softened
- 1 cup mozzarella cheese, shredded
- 1/2 cup bacon bits

Directions
1. Choose the sauté button in the Ninja Foodi.
2. Add the butter.
3. Wait for it to melt.
4. Cook the garlic for 2 min.
5. Add the potatoes and the rest of the ingredients except the milk, cheeses and bacon bits.
6. Seal the pot.
7. Choose pressure.
8. Cook at high pressure for 25 min.
9. Release the pressure naturally.
10. Take the potatoes out and mash with a fork.
11. Stir in the milk and cream cheese.
12. Put back the mashed potatoes.

13. Mix well.
14. Sprinkle the mozzarella and bacon bits on top.

Serving Suggestion: Serve with main course.
Tip: Use a potato masher to make things easier.
Nutrition value/serving: Calories 199, Total Fat 10.3g, Saturated Fat 5.6g, Cholesterol 30mg, Sodium 349mg, Total Carbohydrate 19.8g, Dietary Fiber 2.6g, Total Sugars 3.3g, Protein 7.4g, Potassium 529mg

Minestrone Soup

Prep time: 30 min, Serves: 6
Ingredients
- 2 tablespoons olive oil
- 1 onion, diced
- 3 cloves garlic, minced
- 2 stalks celery, diced
- 2 carrots, peeled and diced
- 1 teaspoon dried oregano
- 1 1/2 teaspoons dried basil
- 1/2 teaspoon fennel seed
- 6 cups chicken broth
- 28 oz. diced tomatoes
- 16 oz. kidney beans, rinsed and drained
- 1 zucchini, chopped
- 1 bay leaf
- 1 cup kale, chopped
- 2 teaspoons red wine vinegar
- Salt and pepper to taste
- 1/4 cup Parmesan cheese, grated

Directions
1. Set the Ninja Foodi to sauté.
2. Add the oil.
3. Cook the onion, garlic, celery and carrots for 3 min.
4. Add the dried herbs and cook for 1 minute.
5. Add the rest of the ingredients except the kale and Parmesan.
6. Choose pressure.
7. Cover the pot.
8. Cook at high pressure for 5 min.
9. Release the pressure quickly.
10. Stir in the kale and wait for it to wilt and sprinkle Parmesan on top before serving.

Serving Suggestion: Garnish with chopped parsley.
Tip: Use low sodium chicken broth.

Nutrition value/serving: Calories 314, Total Fat 6.9g, Saturated Fat 1.9g, Cholesterol 5mg, Sodium 670mg, Total Carbohydrate 44.7g, Dietary Fiber 11.1g, Total Sugars 6.2g, Protein 20.5g, Potassium 1357mg

Tomato Basil Soup

Prep time: 30 min, Serves: 8
Ingredients
- 1 tablespoon olive oil
- 1 cup onion, chopped
- 1 cup celery, chopped
- 1 cup carrot, chopped
- 30 oz. canned diced tomatoes, undrained
- 2 tablespoons tomato paste
- 4 cups chicken broth
- 1/4 cup fresh basil leaves, chopped
- 1 teaspoon dried oregano leaves
- 1/2 cup butter
- Salt and pepper to taste
- 1/2 cup all-purpose flour
- 1 cup Parmesan cheese, grated
- 1-1/2 cups half and half

Directions
1. Set the Ninja Foodi to sauté.
2. Pour in the oil.
3. Add the onion, celery and carrot.
4. Cook for 2 min.
5. Add the rest of the ingredients except the flour, Parmesan and half and half.
6. Seal the pot.
7. Set it to pressure. Cook at high pressure for 5 min.
8. Release the pressure naturally.
9. Pour the soup into a food processor. Pulse until smooth.
10. Pour it back to the pot.
11. Set it to sauté. Add the remaining ingredients.
12. Simmer for 5 min.

Serving Suggestion: Serve with toasted whole wheat bread.
Tip: Use freshly grated Parmesan cheese.
Nutrition value/serving: Calories 271, Total Fat 20.3g, Saturated Fat 11.5g, Cholesterol 50mg, Sodium 544mg, Total Carbohydrate 16.6g, Dietary

Fiber 2.6g, Total Sugars 5.2g, Protein 7.3g, Potassium 570mg

Ham & Potato Soup

Prep time: 30 min, Serves: 4

Ingredients
- 2 tablespoons butter
- 1/2 cup carrots, sliced
- 1 onion, chopped
- 3 cloves garlic, minced
- 2 stalks celery, chopped
- 1 lb. cooked ham, cubed
- 2 lb. potatoes, cubed
- 32 oz. vegetable stock
- 1/4 cup coconut cream
- Salt and pepper to taste
- 1 teaspoon dried thyme

Directions
1. Select the sauté function in the Ninja Foodi.
2. Add the butter, onion, garlic, celery and carrot.
3. Cook for 5 min.
4. Add the rest of the ingredients except the cream.
5. Set it to pressure.
6. Cover the pot.
7. Cook at high pressure for 5 min.
8. Release the pressure quickly.
9. Stir in the cream before serving.

Serving Suggestion: Top with croutons.

Nutrition value/serving: Calories 434, Total Fat 15g, Saturated Fat 8g, Cholesterol 88mg, Sodium 532mg, Total Carbohydrates 51g, Dietary Fiber 4g, Sugars 6g, Protein 24g, Potassium 1430mg

Chapter 7: Snacks, Appetizers & Sides Recipes

Honey Mustard Hot Dogs

Prep time: 22 min, Serves: 4

Ingredients
- 20 Hot Dogs, cut into 4 pieces
- ¼ cup honey
- ¼ cup red wine vinegar
- ½ cup tomato puree
- ¼ cup water
- 1½ teaspoon soy sauce
- 1 teaspoon Dijon mustard
- Salt and black pepper to taste

Directions
1. Add the tomato puree, red wine vinegar, honey, soy sauce, Dijon mustard, salt, and black pepper in a medium bowl. Mix them with a spoon.
2. Put sausage weenies in the crisp basket, and close the crisping lid. Select Air Crisp mode. Set the temperature to 370 ° F and the timer to 4 min. Press Start/Stop. At the 2-minute mark, turn the sausages.
3. Once ready, open the lid and pour the sweet sauce over the sausage weenies.
4. Close the pressure lid, secure the pressure valve, and select Pressure mode on High for 3 min. Press Start/Stop. Once the timer has ended, do a quick pressure release. Serve and enjoy.

Cheesy Tangy Arancini

Prep time: 105 min, Serves: 6

Ingredients
- ½ cup olive oil, plus 1 tablespoon
- 2 large eggs
- 2 garlic cloves, minced
- 1 small white onion; diced
- ½ cup apple cider vinegar
- 2 cups short grain rice
- 2 cups fresh panko bread crumbs
- 5 cups chicken stock
- 1½ cups grated Parmesan cheese, plus more for garnish
- 1 cup chopped green beans
- 1 teaspoon salt
- 1teaspoon freshly ground black pepper

Directions
1. Choose Sear/Sauté on the pot and set to Medium High. Choose Start/Stop to preheat the pot. Add 1 tablespoon of oil and the onion, cook the onion until translucent, add the garlic and cook further for 2 min or until the garlic starts getting fragrant.
2. Stir in the stock, vinegar, and rice. Seal the pressure lid, choose pressure, set to High, and set the time to 7 min; press Start.
3. After cooking, perform a natural pressure release for 10 min, then a quick pressure release and carefully open the pressure lid.
4. Stir in the Parmesan cheese, green beans, salt, and pepper to mash the rice until a risotto forms. Spoon the mixture into a bowl and set aside to cool completely.
5. Clean the pot and in a bowl, combine the breadcrumbs and the remaining olive oil. In another bowl, lightly beat the eggs.
6. Form 12 balls out of the risotto or as many as you can get. Dip each into the beaten eggs, and coat in the breadcrumb mixture.
7. Put half of the rice balls in the Crisping Basket in a single layer. Close the crisping lid, hit Air Crisp, set the temperature to 400°F, and set the time to 10 min; press Start. Leave to cool before serving.

Chicken Wings

Prep time: 60 min, Serves: 4

Ingredients
- 2 lb. chicken wings, frozen
- ½ 1-ounce ranch salad mix
- ½ cup sriracha sauce
- ½ cup water
- 2 tablespoon butter, melted
- 1 tablespoon lemon juice
- ½ teaspoon paprika
- Non-stick cooking spray

Directions

1. Mix the water, sriracha, butter and lemon juice or vinegar in the pot. In the Crisping Basket, put the wings, and then the basket into the pot.
2. Seal the pressure lid, choose Pressure, set to High, set the timer at 5 min, and press Start. When the timer is done reading, perform a quick pressure release, and carefully open the lid.
3. Pour the paprika and ranch dressing all over the chicken and oil with cooking spray. Cover the crisping lid. Choose Air Crisp, set the temperature to 370° F, and the timer to 15 min. Choose Start to commence frying.
4. After half the cooking time, open the lid, remove the basket and shake the wings. Oil the chicken again with cooking spray and return the basket to the pot. Close the lid and continue cooking until the wings are crispy to your desire.

Artichoke Bites

Prep time: 70 min, Serves: 8

Ingredients
- ¼ cup frozen chopped kale
- ¼ cup finely chopped artichoke hearts
- ¼ cup goat cheese
- ¼ cup ricotta cheese
- 4 13-by-18-inch sheets frozen phyllo dough, thawed
- 1 lemon, zested
- 1 large egg white
- 1 tablespoon olive oil
- 2 tablespoons grated Parmesan cheese
- 1 teaspoon dried basil
- ½ teaspoon salt
- ½ teaspoon freshly ground black pepper

Directions
1. In a bowl, mix the kale, artichoke hearts, ricotta cheese, parmesan cheese, goat cheese, egg white, basil, lemon zest, salt, and pepper. Put the Crisping Basket in the pot. Close the crisping lid, choose Air Crisp, set the temperature to 375°F, and the time to 5 min; press Start/Stop.
2. Then, place a phyllo sheet on a clean flat surface. Brush with olive oil, place a second phyllo sheet on the first, and brush with oil. Continue layering to form a pile of four oiled sheets.
3. Working from the short side, cut the phyllo sheets into 8 strips. Cut the strips in half to form 16 strips.
4. Spoon 1 tablespoon of filling onto one short side of every strip. Fold a corner to cover the filling to make a triangle; continue repeatedly folding to the end of the strip, creating a triangle-shaped phyllo packet. Repeat the process with the other phyllo bites.
5. Open the crisping lid and place half of the pastry in the basket in a single layer. Close the lid, Choose Air Crisp, set the temperature to 350°F, and the timer to 12 min; press Start/Stop.
6. After 6 min, open the lid, and flip the bites. Return the basket to the pot and close the lid to continue baking. When ready, take out the bites into a plate. Serve warm.

Zesty Brussels Sprouts with Raisins

Prep time: 45 min, Serves: 4

Ingredients
- 14 oz. Brussels sprouts, steamed
- 2 oz. toasted pine nuts
- 2 oz. raisins
- 1 tablespoon olive oil
- Juice and zest of 1 orange

Directions
1. Soak the raisins in the orange juice and let sit for about 20 min. Drizzle the Brussels sprouts with the olive oil, and place them in the basket of the Ninja Foodi.
2. Close the crisping lid and cook for 15 min on Air Crisp mode at 370° F. Remove to a bowl and top with pine nuts, raisins, and orange zest.

Eggplant Chips with Honey

Prep time: 20 min, Serves: 4

Ingredients
- 2 eggplants
- ⅓ cup cornstarch
- ½ cup water
- ⅓ cup olive oil
- 2 teaspoon honey
- 1 teaspoon dry thyme
- A pinch of salt

Directions

1. Cut the eggplants in slices of ½-inch each. In a big bowl, mix the cornstarch, water, olive oil, and eggplant slices, until evenly coated. Line the Ninja Foodi basket with baking paper and spray with olive oil.
2. Place the eggplants in the basket, scatter with thyme and cook for 15 min on Air Crisp mode, shaking every 5 min at 370° F. When ready, transfer the eggplants to a serving platter and drizzle with honey. Serve with yogurt dip.

Asparagus Wrapped in Prosciutto with Garbanzo Dip.

Prep time: 15 min, Serves: 6

Ingredients
- 1 lb. asparagus, stalks trimmed
- 10 oz. Prosciutto, thinly sliced
- Cooking spray

For the Dip:
- 1 medium onion; diced
- 2 medium jalapeños; chopped
- 2 cloves of garlic, minced
- 1 cup canned garbanzo beans
- 1 cup crushed tomatoes
- 1 cup vegetable broth
- 1 ½ tablespoon olive oil
- 1 teaspoon paprika
- ¾ teaspoon sea salt
- ½ teaspoon chili powder

Directions
1. Open the Ninja Foodi and add the garbanzo beans, onion, jalapeños, garlic, tomatoes, broth, oil, paprika, chili powder, and salt. Close the lid, secure the pressure valve, and select Pressure mode on High for 8 min. Press Start/Stop.
2. Once the timer has ended, do a quick pressure release, and open the pot.
3. Transfer the Ingredients to a food processor, and blend until creamy and smooth. Set aside. Wrap each asparagus with a slice of prosciutto from top to bottom.
4. Grease the crisp basket with cooking spray, and add in the wrapped asparagus.
5. Close the crisping lid, select Air Crisp mode at 370 ° F and set the time to 8 min. Press Start/Stop. At the 4-minute mark, turn the bombs. Remove the wrapped asparagus onto a plate and serve with bean dip.

Cheesy Smashed Sweet Potatoes

Prep time: 70 min, Serves: 4

Ingredients
- 2 slices bacon, cooked and crumbled
- 12 ounces baby sweet potatoes
- ¼ cup shredded Monterey Jack cheese
- ¼ cup sour cream
- 1 tablespoon chopped scallions
- 1 teaspoon melted butter
- Salt to taste

Directions
1. Put the Crisping Basket in the pot and close the crisping lid. Choose Air Crisp, set the temperature to 350°F, and the time to 5 min. Press Start/Stop to begin preheating.
2. Meanwhile, toss the sweet potatoes with the melted butter until evenly coated. Once the pot and basket have preheated, open the lid and add the sweet potatoes to the basket. Close the lid, Choose Air Crisp, set the temperature to 350°F, and set the time to 30 min; press Start.
3. After 15 min, open the lid, pull out the basket and shake the sweet potatoes. Return the basket to the pot and close the lid to continue cooking. When ended, check the sweet potatoes for your desired crispiness, which should also be fork tender.
4. Take out the sweet potatoes from the basket and use a large spoon to crush the soft potatoes just to split lightly. Top with the cheese, sour cream, bacon, and scallions, and season with salt.

Cheesy Cauliflower Tater Tots

Prep time: 35 min, Serves: 10

Ingredients
- 2 lb. cauliflower florets, steamed
- 5 oz. cheddar cheese
- 1 egg, beaten
- 1 onion; diced
- 1 cup breadcrumbs
- 1 teaspoon chopped chives
- 1 teaspoon garlic powder

- 1 teaspoon chopped parsley
- 1 teaspoon chopped oregano
- Salt and pepper, to taste

Directions

1. Mash the cauliflower and place it in a large bowl. Add the onion, parsley, oregano, chives, garlic powder, salt, and pepper, and cheddar cheese. Mix with hands until thoroughly combined.
2. Form 12 balls out of the mixture. Line a baking sheet with paper. Dip half of the tater tots into the egg and then coat with breadcrumbs.
3. Arrange them on the baking sheet, close the crisping lid and cook in the Ninja Foodi at 350° F for 15 min on Air Crisp mode. Repeat with the other half.

Buttery Chicken Meatballs

Prep time: 90 min, Serves: 6

Ingredients

- 1 pound ground chicken
- 1 green bell pepper, minced
- 1 egg
- 2 celery stalks, minced
- ¼ cup hot sauce
- ½ cup water
- ¼ cup panko bread crumbs
- ¼ cup crumbled queso fresco
- 2 tablespoons melted butter

Directions

1. Choose Sear/Sauté on the pot and set to High. Choose Start/Stop to preheat the pot. Meanwhile, in a bowl, evenly combine the chicken, bell pepper, celery, queso fresco, hot sauce, breadcrumbs, and egg. Form meatballs out of the mixture.
2. Then, pour the melted butter into the pot and fry the meatballs in batches until lightly browned on all sides. Use a slotted spoon to remove the meatballs onto a plate.
3. Put the Crisping Basket in the pot. Pour in the water and put all the meatballs in the basket. Seal the pressure lid, choose Pressure, set to High, and set the timer to 5 min. Choose Start/Stop to begin cooking.
4. When done cooking, perform a quick pressure release and carefully open the lid. Close the crisping lid. Choose Air Crisp, set the temperature to 360°F, and set the time to 10 min; press Start.
5. After 5 min, open the lid, lift the basket and shake the meatballs. Return the basket to the pot and close the lid to continue cooking until the meatballs are crispy.

Steak and Minty Cheese

Prep time: 15 min, Serves: 4

Ingredients

- 2 New York strip steaks
- 8 oz. halloumi cheese
- 12 kalamata olives
- Juice and zest of 1 lemon
- Olive oil
- 2 tablespoon chopped parsley
- 2 tablespoon chopped mint
- Salt and pepper, to taste

Directions

1. Season the steaks with salt and pepper, and gently brush with olive oil. Place into the Ninja Foodi, close the crisping lid and cook for 6 min for medium rare on Air Crisp mode at 350° F. When ready, remove to a plate and set aside.
2. Drizzle the cheese with olive oil and place it in the Ninja Foodi; cook for 4 min.
3. Remove to a serving platter and serve with sliced steaks and olives, sprinkled with herbs, and lemon zest and juice.

Barbecue Chicken Drumsticks

Prep time: 30 min, Serves: 6

Ingredients

- 3 lb. chicken drumsticks
- 1 cup Barbecue sauce
- ¼ cup butter, melted
- ½ cup water
- 3 tablespoon garlic powder
- Salt to taste

Directions

1. Season drumsticks with garlic powder and salt. Open the Ninja Foodi, pour in the water, and fit in the reversible rack. Arrange the drumsticks on top, close the lid, secure the pressure valve, and

select Pressure mode for 5 min. Press Start/Stop to start cooking.
2. Once the timer has ended, do a natural pressure release for 10 min, and then a quick pressure release to let out any more steam. Open the lid.
3. Remove the drumsticks to a crisp basket and add the butter and half of the barbecue sauce. Stir the chicken until well coated in the sauce.
4. Insert the basket in the pot and close the crisping lid. Select Air Crisp, set to 380 ° F, and cook for 10 min. Select Start/Stop. Once nice and crispy, remove drumsticks to a bowl, and top with the remaining barbecue sauces. Stir and serve the chicken with a cheese dip.

Teriyaki Chicken Wings

Prep time: 30 min
Serves: 6

Ingredients
- 2 lb. chicken wings
- 1 cup teriyaki sauce
- 1 tablespoon honey
- 2 tablespoon cornstarch
- 2 tablespoon cold water
- 1 teaspoon finely ground black pepper
- 1 teaspoon sesame seeds

Directions
1. In the pot, combine honey, teriyaki sauce and black pepper until the honey dissolves completely; toss in chicken to coat. Seal the pressure lid, choose Pressure, set to High, and set the timer to 10 min. Press Start.
2. When ready, release the pressure quickly. Transfer chicken wings to a platter. Mix cold water with the cornstarch.
3. Press Sear/Sauté and stir in cornstarch slurry into the sauce and cook for 3 to 5 min until thickened. Top the chicken with thickened sauce. Add a garnish of sesame seeds, and serve.

Sweet Pickled Cucumbers

Prep time: 5 min, Serves: 6

Ingredients
- 1 pound small cucumbers; sliced into rings
- 1/4 cup green garlic, minced
- 2 cups white vinegar
- 1 cup sugar
- 1 cup water
- 2 tablespoon Dill Pickle Seasoning
- 2 teaspoon salt
- 1 teaspoon cumin

Directions
1. Into the pot, add sliced cucumber, vinegar and pour water on top. Sprinkle sugar over cucumbers. Add cumin, dill pickle seasoning, and salt.
2. Stir well to dissolve the sugar. Seal the pressure lid, choose Pressure, set to High, and set the timer to 4 min. Press Start.
3. When ready, release the pressure quickly. Ladle cucumbers into a large storage container and pour cooking liquid over the top. Chill for 1 hour.

Fried Beef Dumplings

Prep time: 45 min, Serves: 8

Ingredients
- 8 ounces ground beef
- 20 wonton wrappers
- 1 carrot, grated
- 1 large egg, beaten
- 1 garlic clove, minced
- ½ cup grated cabbage
- 2 tablespoons olive oil
- 2 tablespoons coconut aminos
- ½ tablespoon melted ghee
- ½ tablespoon ginger powder
- ½ teaspoon salt
- ½ teaspoon freshly ground black pepper

Directions
1. Put the Crisping Basket in the pot. Close the crisping lid, choose Air Crisp, set the temperature to 400°F, and the time to 5 min; press Start/Stop. In a large bowl, mix the beef, cabbage, carrot, egg, garlic, coconut aminos, ghee, ginger, salt, and black pepper.
2. Put the wonton wrappers on a clean flat surface and spoon 1 tablespoon of the beef mixture into the middle of each wrapper.
3. Run the edges of the wrapper with a little water; fold the wrapper to cover the filling into a semi-circle shape and pinch the edges to seal. Brush the dumplings with olive oil.

4. Lay the dumplings in the preheated basket, choose Air Crisp, set the temperature to 400°F, and set the time to 12 min. Choose Start/Stop to begin frying.
5. After 6 min, open the lid, pull out the basket and shake the dumplings. Return the basket to the pot and close the lid to continue frying until the dumplings are crispy to your desire.

Crispy Cheesy Straws

Prep time: 45 min, Serves: 8

Ingredients
- 2 cups cauliflower florets, steamed
- 5 oz. cheddar cheese
- 3 ½ oz. oats
- 1 egg
- 1 red onion; diced
- 1 teaspoon mustard
- Salt and pepper, to taste

Directions
1. Add the oats in a food processor and process until they resemble breadcrumbs. Place the steamed florets in a cheesecloth and squeeze out the excess liquid.
2. Put the florets in a large bowl, and add the rest of the Ingredients to the bowl.
3. Mix well with your hands, to combine the Ingredients thoroughly.
4. Take a little bit of the mixture and twist it into a straw. Place in the lined Ninja Foodi basket; repeat with the rest of the mixture.
5. Close the crisping lid and cook for 10 min on Air Crisp mode at 350° F. After 5 min, turn them over and cook for an additional 10 min.

Herby Fish Skewers

Prep time: 75 min, Serves: 4

Ingredients
- 1 pound cod loin, boneless, skinless; cubed
- 2 garlic cloves, grated
- 1 lemon, juiced and zested
- 1 lemon, cut in wedges to serve
- 3 tablespoon olive oil
- 1 teaspoon dill; chopped
- 1 teaspoon parsley; chopped
- Salt to taste

Directions
1. In a bowl, combine the olive oil, garlic, dill, parsley, salt, and lemon juice. Stir in the cod and place in the fridge to marinate for 1 hour. Thread the cod pieces onto halved skewers.
2. Arrange into the oiled Ninja Foodi basket; close the crisping lid and cook for 10 min at 390° F. Flip them over halfway through cooking. When ready, remove to a serving platter, scatter lemon zest and serve with wedges.

Cheesy Cabbage Side Dish

Prep time: 30 min, Serves: 4

Ingredients
- ½ head of cabbage, cut into 4 wedges
- 2 cup Parmesan cheese
- 4 tablespoon butter, melted
- 1 teaspoon smoked paprika
- Salt and pepper, to taste

Directions
1. Line the basket with parchment paper. Brush the butter over the cabbage wedges; season with salt and pepper. Coat the cabbage with the Parmesan cheese. Arrange in the basket and sprinkle with paprika.
2. Close the crisping lid and cook for 15 min on Air Crisp mode, flip over and cook for an additional 10 min; at 330 F.

Fried Pin Wheels

Prep time: 50 min, Serves: 6

Ingredients
- 1 sheet puff pastry
- 1 ½ cups Gruyere cheese, grated
- 8 ham slices
- 4 teaspoon Dijon mustard

Directions
1. Place the pastry on a lightly floured flat surface. Brush the mustard over and arrange the ham slices; top with cheese. Start at the shorter edge and roll up the pastry.
2. Wrap it in a plastic foil and place in the freezer for about half an hour, until it becomes firm and comfortable to cut.

3. Meanwhile, slice the pastry into 6 rounds. Line the Ninja Foodi basket with parchment paper, and arrange the pinwheels on top.
4. Close the crisping lid and cook for 10 min on Air Crisp mode at 370° F. Leave to cool on a wire rack before serving.

Creamy Tomato Parsley Dip

Prep time: 18 min, Serves: 6
Ingredients
- 10 oz. shredded Parmesan cheese
- 10 oz. cream cheese
- ½ cup heavy cream
- 1 cup chopped tomatoes
- 1 cup water
- ¼ cup chopped parsley

Directions
1. Open the Ninja Foodi and pour in the tomatoes, parsley, heavy cream, cream cheese, and water. Close the lid, secure the pressure valve, and select Pressure for 3 min at High. Press Start/Stop.
2. Once the timer has ended, do a natural pressure release for 10 min.
3. Stir the mixture with a spoon while mashing the tomatoes with the back of the spoon. Add the parmesan cheese and Close the crisping lid.
4. Select Bake/Roast mode, set the temperature to 370 ° F and the time to 3 min. Dish the dip into a bowl and serve with chips or veggie bites.

Turkey Scotch Eggs

Prep time: 20 min, Serves: 6
Ingredients
- 10 oz. ground turkey
- 4 eggs, soft boiled, peeled
- 2 garlic cloves, minced
- 2 eggs, lightly beaten
- 1 white onion; chopped
- ½ cup flour
- ½ cup breadcrumbs
- 1 teaspoon dried mixed herbs
- Salt and pepper to taste
- Cooking spray

Directions
1. Mix together the onion, garlic, salt, and pepper. Shape into 4 balls. Wrap the turkey mixture around each egg, and ensure the eggs are well covered.
2. Dust each egg ball in flour, then dip in the beaten eggs and finally roll in the crumbs, until coated. Spray with cooking spray.
3. Lay the eggs into your Ninja Foodi's basket. Set the temperature to 390 ° F, close the crisping lid and cook for 15 min. After 8 min, turn the eggs. Slice in half and serve warm.

Cheesy Tomato Bruschetta

Prep time: 15 min, Serves: 2
Ingredients
- 1 Italian Ciabatta Sandwich Bread
- 2 tomatoes; chopped
- 2 garlic cloves, minced
- 1 cup grated mozzarella cheese
- Olive oil to brush
- Basil leaves; chopped
- Salt and pepper to taste

Directions
1. Cut the bread in half, lengthways, then each piece again in half. Drizzle each bit with olive oil and sprinkle with garlic. Top with the grated cheese, salt, and pepper.
2. Place the bruschetta pieces into the Ninja Foodi basket, close the crisping lid and cook for 12 min on Air Crisp mode at 380° F. At 6 min, check for doneness.
3. Once the Ninja Foodi beeps, remove the bruschetta to a serving platter, spoon over the tomatoes and chopped basil to serve.

Rosemary Potato Fries

Prep time: 30 min, Serves: 4
Ingredients
- 4 russet potatoes, cut into sticks
- 2 garlic cloves, crushed
- 2 tablespoon butter, melted
- 1 teaspoon fresh rosemary; chopped
- Salt and pepper, to taste

Directions
1. Add butter, garlic, salt, and pepper to a bowl; toss until the sticks are well-coated. Lay the

potato sticks into the Ninja Foodi's basket. Close the crisping lid and cook for 15 min at 370° F. Shake the potatoes every 5 min.
2. Once ready, check to ensure the fries are golden and crispy all over if not, return them to cook for a few min.
3. Divide standing up between metal cups lined with nonstick baking paper, and serve sprinkled with rosemary.

Rosemary and Garlic Mushrooms

Prep time: 20 min, Serves: 4

Ingredients
- 12 oz. button mushrooms
- 2 rosemary sprigs
- 3 garlic cloves, minced
- ¼ cup melted butter
- ½ teaspoon salt
- ¼ teaspoon black pepper

Directions
1. Wash and pat dry the mushrooms and cut them in half. Place in a large bowl. Add the remaining Ingredients to the bowl and toss well to combine.
2. Transfer the mushrooms to the basket of the Ninja Foodi. Close the crisping lid and cook for 12 min on Air Crisp mode, shaking once halfway through; at 350° F.

Chicken Meatballs with Ranch Dip

Prep time: 34 min, Serves: 4

Ingredients
- 1 lb. ground chicken
- 1 egg, beaten
- Green onions for garnish
- 2 tablespoon minced garlic
- 2 tablespoon olive oil
- 2 tablespoon chopped green onions
- 5 tablespoon Hot sauce
- 2 tablespoon Buffalo wing sauce
- Salt and pepper, to taste

For the dip:
- ½ cup Roquefort cheese, crumbled
- 2 tablespoon olive oil
- 2 tablespoon mayonnaise
- ¼ tablespoon heavy cream
- Juice from ½ lemon

Directions
1. Mix all salsa Ingredients in a bowl until uniform and creamy, and refrigerate. Add the ground chicken, salt, garlic, and two tablespoons of green onions. Mix well with your hands.
2. Rub your hands with some oil and form bite-size balls out of the mixture. Lay onto your crisp basket fryer basket. Spray with cooking spray.
3. Select Air Crisp, set the temperature to 385 ° F and the time to 14min. At the 7-minute mark, turn the meatballs.
4. Meanwhile, add the hot sauce and butter to a bowl and microwave them until the butter melts. Mix the sauce with a spoon.
5. Pour the hot sauce mixture and a half cup of water over the meatballs.
6. Close the lid, secure the pressure valve, and select Sear/Sauté mode on High Pressure for 10 min. Press Start/Stop.
7. Once the timer has ended, do a quick pressure release. Dish the meatballs. Garnish with green onions, and serve with Roquefort sauce.

Cheesy Brazilian Balls

Prep time: 35 min, Serves: 4

Ingredients
- 2 cups flour
- 2 cups grated mozzarella cheese
- ½ cup olive oil
- 1 cup milk
- 2 eggs, cracked into a bowl
- A pinch of salt

Directions
1. Grease the crisp basket with cooking spray and set aside. Put the Ninja Foodi on Medium and select Sear/Sauté mode. Add the milk, oil, and salt, and let boil. Add the flour and mix it vigorously with a spoon.
2. Let the mixture cool. Once cooled, use a hand mixer to mix the dough well, and add the eggs and cheese while still mixing. The dough should be thick and sticky.
3. Use your hands to make 14 balls out of the mixture, and put them in the greased basket. Put the basket in the pot and close the crisping lid.

4. Select Air Crisp, set the temperature to 380 ° F and set the timer to 15 min. At the 7-minute mark, shake the balls. Serve with lemon aioli, garlic mayo or ketchup.

Cheesy Bacon Dip

Prep time: 10 min, Serves: 10
Ingredients
- 10 bacon slices; chopped roughly
- 4 chopped tomatoes
- 1 cup water
- 1¼ cup cream cheese
- 1¼ cup shredded Monterey Jack cheese

Directions
1. Turn on the Ninja Foodi and select Air Crisp mode. Set the temperature to 370 ° F and the time to 8 min. Add the bacon pieces and close the crisping lid. Press Start/Stop.
2. When ready, open the lid and add the water, cream cheese, and tomatoes. Do Not Stir. Close the lid, secure the pressure valve, and select Pressure mode on High for 5 min. Press Start/Stop.
3. Once the timer has ended, do a quick pressure release, and open the lid. Stir in the cheddar cheese and mix to combine. Serve with a side of chips.

Cheese bombs wrapped in Bacon.

Prep time: 20 min, Serves: 8
Ingredients
- 8 bacon slices, cut in half
- 16 oz. Mozzarella cheese, cut into 8 pieces
- 3 tablespoon butter, melted

Directions
1. Wrap each cheese string with a slice of bacon and secure the ends with toothpicks. Set aside. Grease the crisp basket with the melted butter and add in the bombs.
2. Close the crisping lid, select Air Crisp mode, and set the temperature to 370 ° F and set the time to 10 min.
3. At the 5-minute mark, turn the bombs. When ready, remove to a paper-lined plate to drain the excess oil. Serve on a platter with toothpicks and tomato dip.

Spinach Hummus

Prep time: 1 hr 10 min, Serves: 12
Ingredients
- 2 cups spinach; chopped
- ½ cup tahini
- 2 cups dried chickpeas
- 8 cups water
- 5 garlic cloves, crushed
- 5 tablespoon grapeseed oil
- 2 teaspoon salt; divided
- 5 tablespoon lemon juice

Directions
1. In the pressure cooker, mix 2 tablespoon oil, water, 1 teaspoon salt, and chickpeas. Seal the pressure lid, choose Pressure, set to High, and set the timer to 35 min. Press Start. When ready, release the pressure quickly. In a small bowl, reserve ½ cup of the cooking liquid and drain chickpeas.
2. Mix half the reserved cooking liquid and chickpeas in a food processor and puree until no large chickpeas remain; add remaining cooking liquid, spinach, lemon juice, remaining teaspoon salt, garlic, and tahini.
3. Process hummus for 8 min until smooth. Stir in the remaining 3 tablespoon of olive oil before serving.

Egg Brulee

Prep time: 12 min, Serves: 8
Ingredients
- 8 large eggs
- 1 cup water
- Salt to taste
- Ice bath

Directions
1. Open the Ninja Foodi, pour the water in, and fit the reversible rack in it. Put the eggs on the rack in a single layer, close the lid, secure the pressure valve, and select Pressure on High Pressure for 5 min. Press Start/Stop.
2. Once the timer has ended, do a quick pressure release, and open the pot.

3. Remove the eggs into the ice bath and peel the eggs. Put the peeled eggs in a plate and slice them in half.
4. Sprinkle a bit of salt on them and then followed by the sugar. Lay onto your crisp basket fryer basket. Select Air Crisp mode, set the temperature to 390 ° F and the time to 3 min.

Cumin Baby Carrots

Prep time: 25 min, Serves: 4

Ingredients
- 1 ¼ lb. baby carrots
- 1 handful cilantro; chopped
- 2 tablespoon olive oil
- ½ teaspoon cumin powder
- ½ teaspoon garlic powder
- 1 teaspoon cumin seeds
- 1 teaspoon salt
- ½ teaspoon black pepper

Directions
1. Place the baby carrots in a large bowl. Add cumin seeds, cumin, olive oil, salt, garlic powder, and pepper, and stir to coat them well.
2. Put the carrots in the Ninja Foodi's basket, close the crisping lid and cook for 20 min on Roast mode at 370° F. Remove to a platter and sprinkle with chopped cilantro, to serve.

Wrapped Asparagus in Bacon

Prep time: 30 min, Serves: 6

Ingredients
- 1 lb. bacon; sliced
- 1 lb. asparagus spears, trimmed
- ½ cup Parmesan cheese, grated
- Cooking spray
- Salt and pepper, to taste

Directions
1. Place the bacon slices out on a work surface, top each one with one asparagus spear and half of the cheese. Wrap the bacon around the asparagus.
2. Line the Ninja Foodi basket with parchment paper. Arrange the wraps into the basket, scatter over the remaining cheese, season with salt and black pepper, and spray with cooking spray. Close the crisping lid and cook for 8 to 10 min on Roast mode at 370° F. If necessary work in batches. Serve hot!

Mouthwatering Meatballs

Prep time: 30 min, Serves: 6

Ingredients
- 2 lb. ground beef
- 1 potato, shredded
- 2 eggs, beaten
- ½ cup Parmesan cheese, grated
- 2 cups tomato sauce to serve
- 2 tablespoon chopped chives
- ¼ teaspoon pepper
- ½ teaspoon garlic powder
- ½ teaspoon salt
- 1 package cooked spaghetti to serve
- Basil leaves to serve
- Cooking spray

Directions
1. In a large bowl, combine the potato, salt, pepper, garlic powder, eggs, and chives. Form 12 balls out of the mixture. Spray with cooking spray. Arrange half of the balls onto a lined Ninja Foodi basket.
2. Close the crisping lid and cook for 14 min on Air Crisp mode at 330 F. After 7 min, turn the meatballs.
3. Repeat with the other half. Serve over cooked spaghetti mixed with tomato sauce, sprinkled with Parmesan cheese and basil leaves.

Green Vegan Dip

Prep time: 20 min, Serves: 4

Ingredients
- 10 ounces canned green chiles, drained with liquid reserved
- 2 cups broccoli florets
- ¼ cup raw cashews
- ¼ cup soy sauce
- 1 cup water
- ¾ cup green bell pepper; chopped
- ¼ teaspoon garlic powder
- ½ teaspoon sea salt
- ¼ teaspoon chili powder

Directions

1. In the cooker, add cashews, broccoli, green bell pepper, and water. Seal the pressure lid, choose Pressure, set to High, and set the timer to 5 min. Press Start. When ready, release the pressure quickly.
2. Drain water from the pot; add reserved liquid from canned green chilies, sea salt, garlic powder, chili powder, soy sauce, and cumin.
3. Use an immersion blender to blend the mixture until smooth; set aside in a mixing bowl. Stir green chilies through the dip; add your desired optional additions.

Chicken and Cheese Bake

Prep time: 1 hour 18 min, Serves: 6

Ingredients
- 1 lb. chicken breast
- 10 oz. Cheddar cheese
- 10 oz. cream cheese
- ½ cup sour cream
- ½ cup breadcrumbs
- ½ cup water

Directions
1. Open the Ninja Foodi and add the chicken, water, and cream cheese. Close the lid, secure the pressure valve, and select Pressure mode on High for 10 min. Press Start/Stop.
2. Once the timer has ended, do a quick pressure release, and open the pot.
3. Shred the chicken with two forks and add the cheddar cheese. Sprinkle with breadcrumbs, and close the crisping lid. Select Bake/Roast, set the temperature to 380 ° F and the timer to 3 min. Serve warm with veggie bites.

Chapter 8: Desserts Recipes

Ginger Cookies

Prep time: 10 min, Cooking time: 14 min, Serves: 7

Ingredients

- 1 cup almond flour
- 3 tablespoons butter
- 1 egg
- ½ teaspoon baking powder
- 3 tablespoon Erythritol
- 1 teaspoon ground ginger
- ½ teaspoon ground cinnamon
- 3 tablespoons heavy cream

Directions

1. Beat the egg in the bowl and whisk it gently.
2. Add baking powder, Erythritol, ground ginger, ground cinnamon, heavy cream, and flour.
3. Stir gently and add butter,
4. Knead the non-sticky dough.
5. Roll up the dough with the help of the rolling pin and make the cookies with the help of the cutter.
6. Place the cookies in the basket in one layer and close the lid.
7. Set the Bake mode and cook the cookies for 14 min at 350 F.
8. When the cookies are cooked – let them chill well and serve!

Nutrition value/serving: calories 172, fat 15.6, fiber 1.8, carbs 4.1, protein 4.4

Vanilla Creme Brulee

Prep time: 20 min, Cooking time: 10 min, Serves: 3

Ingredients

- 1 cup heavy cream
- 4 egg yolks
- 3 tablespoons Truvia
- ½ teaspoon vanilla extract

Directions

1. Whisk together the egg yolks and 2 tablespoons of Truvia.
2. Add heavy cream and stir until homogenous.
3. Place the mixture into the ramekins and cover them with the foil.
4. Make the small holes on the top of the foil with the help of the toothpick.
5. Pour ½ cup of water in Ninja Foofi basket and insert trivet.
6. Place the ramekins on the trivet and close the pressure cooker lid.
7. Cook the dessert on Pressure mode (High pressure) for 10 min.
8. Then make the quick pressure release for 5 min.
9. Let the dessert chill for 10 min.
10. Remove the foil from the ramekins and sprinkle the surface of creme brulee with Truvia.
11. Use the hand torch to caramelize the surface.
12. Serve it!

Nutrition value/serving: calories 212, fat 20.8, fiber 0, carbs 6.7, protein 4.4

Pecan Muffins

Prep time: 10 min, Cooking time: 12 min, Serves: 6

Ingredients

- 4 tablespoon butter, softened
- 4 tablespoon coconut flour
- 1 egg, whisked
- 4 tablespoon heavy cream
- ½ teaspoon vanilla extract
- 1 tablespoon pecans, crushed
- 2 tablespoon Erythritol

Directions

1. In the mixing bowl combine together the coconut flour, softened butter, whisked egg, heavy cream, vanilla extract, and Erythritol.
2. Use the hand mixer to mix up the mixture until smooth.
3. Pour the smooth batter in the silicone muffin molds.
4. Top every muffin with the pecans and transfer in Ninja Foodi rack.
5. Lower the air fryer lid and set Bake mode.
6. Cook the muffins for 12 min at 350 F.

7. Check if the muffins are cooked and transfer on the plate. Chill well and serve!

Nutrition value/serving: calories 170, fat 15.1, fiber 3.6, carbs 11.1, protein 2.8

Vanilla Muffins

Prep time: 7 min, Cooking time: 2 min, Serves: 4

Ingredients

- 4 tablespoon coconut flour
- 1 teaspoon coconut shred
- 1 teaspoon vanilla extract
- 1 egg, beaten
- 1 tablespoon Truvia
- ¼ teaspoon baking powder
- 1 cup water, for cooking

Directions

1. Mix up together all the ingredients and stir well until you get a thick batter.
2. Add water in the Ninja Foodi basket.
3. Place the batter into the muffin molds and transfer them on the Ninja Foodi rack.
4. Lower the pressure cooker lid and set Pressure mode (High pressure).
5. Cook the muffins for 2 min. Use the quick pressure release method.
6. Chill the muffins and serve!

Nutrition value/serving: calories 61, fat 2.9, fiber 3.3, carbs 7, protein 2.5

Sweet Zucchini Crisp

Prep time: 5 min, Cooking time: 10 min, Serves: 4

Ingredients

- 1 zucchini, chopped
- 1 teaspoon Vanilla extract
- 2 tablespoon Erythritol
- 1 tablespoon coconut flakes
- 2 tablespoon butter
- 1 tablespoon almond flour

Directions

1. Preheat Ninja Foodi at Sauté/Stear mode for 5 min at 360 F.
2. Toss the butter in the Ninja Foodi basket.
3. Add chopped zucchini and Sauté the vegetables for 3 min.
4. Add vanilla extract, coconut flakes, Erythritol, and stir well.
5. Cook the zucchini for 4 min more.
6. Then add almond flour and stir well.
7. Sauté the dessert for 1 minute.
8. Use the Air crips mode for 2 min to get a crunchy crust.
9. Serve the cooked dessert immediately!

Nutrition value/serving: calories 84, fat 8.5, fiber 0.5, carbs 6.1, protein 0.3

Keto Brownie Batter

Prep time: 10 min, Cooking time: 5 min, Serves: 5

Ingredients

- 1/3 cup almond flour
- 1 tablespoon Erythritol
- ¼ cup heavy cream
- ½ teaspoon vanilla extract
- 3 tablespoons cocoa powder
- 3 tablespoons butter
- 1 oz dark chocolate

Directions

1. Place the almond flour in the springform pan and flatten to make the layer.
2. Then place the springform pan in the pot and lower the air fryer lid.
3. Cook the almond flour for 3 min at 400 F or until the almond flour gets a golden color.
4. Meanwhile, combine together cocoa powder and heavy cream; whisk the heavy cream until smooth.
5. Add vanilla extract and Erythritol.
6. Remove the almond flour from Ninja Foodi and chill well.
7. Toss butter and dark chocolate in the pot and preheat for 1 minute on Sauté/Stear mode.
8. When the butter is soft – add it in the heavy cream mixture.
9. Then add chocolate and almond flour.
10. Stir the mass until homogenous and serve!

Nutrition value/serving: calories 159, fat 14.9, fiber 2.1, carbs 9, protein 2.5

Mint Cake

Prep time: 8 min, Cooking time: 62 min, Serves: 6

Ingredients

- 1 teaspoon dried mint
- 1 cup coconut flour
- 1 teaspoon baking powder
- ¼ cup Erythritol
- 2 eggs, whisked
- ¼ cup heavy cream
- 1 tablespoon butter
- ½ teaspoon lemon zest, grated

Directions

1. In the mixing bowl mix up together all the ingredients.
2. Use the cooking machine to make the soft batter from the mixture.
3. Pour the batter in the Ninja Foodie basket and flatten it well.
4. Close the pressure cooker lid and set Pressure mode. Seal the lid.
5. Cook the cake on Low pressure for 55 min.
6. Then lower the air fryer lid and set Air Crisp mode.
7. Cook the cake for 7 min more at 400 F.
8. Chill the cake well and serve!

Nutrition value/serving: calories 136, fat 7.2, fiber 8.1, carbs 22, protein 4.7

Chocolate Cakes

Prep time: 10 min, Cooking time: 22 min, Serves: 3

Ingredients

- 1 tablespoon cocoa powder
- 4 tablespoons almond flour
- ½ teaspoon vanilla extract
- 1 tablespoon Truvia
- 1/3 cup heavy cream
- ¼ teaspoon baking powder
- Cooking spray

Directions

1. Mix up together the cocoa powder, almond flour, vanilla extract, Truvia, heavy cream, and baking powder.
2. Use the mixer to make the smooth batter.
3. Spray the silicone molds with the cooking spray inside.
4. Pour the batter into the silicone molds and transfer then in Ninja Foodi basket.
5. Close the air fryer lid and set Bake-Roast Option.
6. Cook the cakes at 255 F for 22 min.
7. Serve the dessert chilled!

Nutrition value/serving: calories 108, fat 9.6, fiber 1.6, carbs 5.2, protein 2.6

Pumpkin Pie

Prep time: 10 min, Cooking time: 25 min, Serves: 6

Ingredients

- 1 tablespoon pumpkin puree
- 1 cup coconut flour
- ½ teaspoon baking powder
- 1 teaspoon apple cider vinegar
- 1 teaspoon Pumpkin spices
- 1 tablespoon butter
- ¼ cup heavy cream
- 2 tablespoon liquid stevia
- 1 egg, whisked

Directions

1. Melt the butter and combine it together with the heavy cream, apple cider vinegar, liquid stevia, egg, and baking powder.
2. Add pumpkin puree and coconut flour.
3. After this, add pumpkin spices and stir the batter until smooth.
4. Pour the batter in Ninja Foodi basket and lower the air fryer lid.
5. Set the "Bake" mode 360 F.
6. Cook the pie for 25 min.
7. When the time is over – let the pie chill till the room temperature. Serve it!

Nutrition value/serving: calories 127, fat 6.6, fiber 8.1, carbs 14.2, protein 3.8

Cinnamon Bun

Prep time: 10 min, Cooking time: 15 min, Serves: 8

Ingredients

- 1 cup almond flour
- ½ teaspoon baking powder
- 3 tablespoon Erythritol
- 2 tablespoon ground cinnamon
- ½ teaspoon vanilla extract
- 1 tablespoon butter
- 1 egg, whisked
- ¾ teaspoon salt
- ¼ cup almond milk

Directions

1. Mix up together the almond flour, baking powder, vanilla extract, egg, salt, and almond milk.
2. Knead the soft and non-sticky dough.
3. Roll up the dough with the help of the rolling pin.
4. Sprinkle dough with the butter, cinnamon, and Erythritol.
5. Roll the dough into the log.
6. Cut the roll into 7 pieces.
7. Spray Ninja Foodi basket with the cooking spray.
8. Place the cinnamon buns in the basket and close the lid.
9. Set the Bake mode and cook the buns for 15 min at 355 F.
10. Check if the buns are cooked with the help of the toothpick.
11. Chill the buns well and serve!

Nutrition value/serving: calories 127, fat 10.5, fiber 3, carbs 9.2, protein 4

Chip Cookies

Prep time: 10 min, Cooking time: 9 min, Serves: 8

Ingredients

- 1 oz sugar-free chocolate chips
- 3 tablespoon butter
- 1 cup almond flour
- 1 egg, whisked
- 2 tablespoons Erythritol

Directions

1. Mix up together the almond flour and whisked the egg.
2. Add butter and Erythritol, and mix up the mixture until homogenous.
3. Add chocolate chips and knead the homogenous dough.
4. Make 8 small balls from the dough and transfer them on the rack of Ninja Foodi.
5. Close the air fryer lid and set Bake mode.
6. Cook the chip cookies for 9 min at 360 F.
7. Chill the cookies and serve!

Nutrition value/serving: calories 145, fat 12.3, fiber 1.5, carbs 8.4, protein 3.9

Cinnamon Bites

Prep time: 10 min, Cooking time: 12 min, Serves: 5

Ingredients

- 1 teaspoon ground cinnamon
- 1 cup almond flour
- ½ teaspoon baking powder
- 1 teaspoon olive oil
- ¼ cup almond milk
- 1 teaspoon butter
- ½ teaspoon vanilla extract
- 1 cup water, for cooking

Directions

1. Combine together all the dry ingredients.
2. Then add butter and almond milk in the dry ingredients.
3. Add vanilla extract and olive oil and knead the smooth and non-sticky dough.
4. Make the medium balls from the dough and place them in the silicone molds.
5. Pour water in Ninja Foodi basket.
6. Place the molds on the rack in Ninja Foodi.
7. Close the lid and seal it.
8. Set Pressure mode (High pressure)
9. Cook the cinnamon bites for 10 min.
10. Then make natural pressure release for 10 min.
11. Then remove the liquid from the basket and lower the air fryer lid.
12. Set Air Crisp and cook the bites for 2 min more.
13. Serve !

Nutrition value/serving: calories 180, fat 15.2, fiber 2.9, carbs 6.1, protein 5.1

Keto Brownie

Prep time: 10 min, Cooking time: 32 min, Serves: 6

Ingredients

- 3 tablespoons Truvia
- 1 oz sugar-free chocolate chips
- 2 eggs, whisked
- ½ teaspoon vanilla extract
- 3 tablespoon butter, melted
- 1 tablespoon almond flour

Directions

1. Whisk together the melted butter, almond flour, vanilla extract, and Truvia.
2. Melt the chocolate chips and add them in the butter mixture.
3. Add eggs and stir until smooth.
4. Pour the batter into Ninja Foodi basket (Bake mode) and cook at 360 F for 32 min.
5. Then check if the brownie cooked and chill well.
6. Cut it into the servings and serve!

Nutrition value/serving: calories 99, fat 8.8, fiber 0.1, carbs 5.9, protein 2.4

Keto Donuts

Prep time: 20 min, Cooking time: 10 min, Serves: 5

Ingredients

- 1 ½ cup almond flour
- ½ teaspoon baking soda
- 1 teaspoon vanilla extract
- 1 egg, whisked
- 2 tablespoons Erythritol
- ½ cup heavy cream

Directions

1. Mix up together the whisked egg, heavy cream, Erythritol, vanilla extract, and baking soda.
2. When the mixture is homogenous – add almond flour. Stir well and knead the non-sticky dough.
3. Let the dough rest for 10 min.
4. After this, roll up the dough with the help of the rolling pin into 1 inch thick.
5. Then make the donuts with the help of the cutter.
6. Set the Ninja Foodi Bake mode + Roast option and set 360 F.
7. When the appliance is preheated – place the donuts in the basket and lower the air fryer lid.
8. Cook the donuts for 5 min.
9. Chill the donuts well and serve!

Nutrition value/serving: calories 118, fat 11.5, fiber 1, carbs 2.4, protein 2.7

Pumpkin Muffins

Prep time: 7 min, Cooking time: 20 min, Serves: 5

Ingredients

- 1 tablespoon butter, melted
- 1 tablespoon pumpkin puree
- 1 teaspoon ground cinnamon
- ¼ teaspoon ground ginger
- 1 egg, beaten
- 3 tablespoon Erythritol
- ½ cup almond flour
- ½ teaspoon baking powder

Directions

1. Mix up together all the ingredients in the mixing bowl.
2. Stir the mixture well until smooth.
3. Transfer the mixture into the silicone muffin molds and place on the track in Ninja Foodi.
4. Lower the air fryer lid and set Bake mode.
5. Cook the muffins for 20 min at 330 F.
6. When the time is over – let the muffins rest little and serve!

Nutrition value/serving: calories 52, fat 4.6, fiber 0.7, carbs 8.7, protein 1.8

Avocado Mousse

Prep time: 10 min, Cooking time: 2 min, Serves: 7

Ingredients

- 2 avocado, peeled, cored
- 1 teaspoon of cocoa powder
- 1/3 cup heavy cream
- 1 teaspoon butter
- 3 tablespoons Erythritol

- 1 teaspoon vanilla extract

Directions

1. Preheat Ninja Foodi at "Sauté/Stear" mode for 5 min.
2. Meanwhile, mash the avocado until smooth and mix it up with Erythritol.
3. Place the butter in the pot and melt.
4. Add mashed avocado mixture and stir well.
5. Add cocoa powder and stir until homogenous. Sauté the mixture for 3 min.
6. Meanwhile, whisk the heavy cream on high speed for 2 min.
7. Transfer the cooked avocado mash in the bowl and chill in ice water.
8. When the avocado mash reaches room temperature – add whisked heavy cream and vanilla extract. Stir gently to get white-chocolate swirls.
9. Transfer the mousse into small cups and chill for 4 hours in the fridge.
10. Serve!

Nutrition value/serving: calories 144, fat 13.9, fiber 3.9, carbs 10.5, protein 1.3

Lava Cups

Prep time: 6 min, Cooking time: 8 min, Serves: 2

Ingredients

- 2 eggs, whisked
- 3 tablespoons flax meal
- 2 teaspoon of cocoa powder
- ½ teaspoon baking powder
- 2 tablespoons heavy cream
- Cooking spray

Directions

1. Spray the cake cups with the cooking spray inside.
2. Mix up together all the remaining ingredients and pour the mixture into the prepared cups.
3. Cover the cups with foil and place in Ninja Foodi.
4. Set the Bake mode 355 F.
5. Close the lid and cook the dessert for 8 min.
6. Serve the cooked lava cups hot!

Nutrition value/serving: calories 165, fat 13.9, fiber 3.6, carbs 5.3, protein 8.4

Mini Cheesecakes

Prep time: 30 min
Cooking time: 4 min
Serves: 4

Ingredients

- 8 tablespoons cream cheese
- 4 tablespoon Erythritol
- 2 tablespoons heavy cream
- ½ teaspoon vanilla extract
- 4 tablespoons almond flour

Directions

1. Whisk together the cream cheese and heavy cream.
2. When the mixture is smooth – add 1 tablespoon of Erythritol and stir until homogenous.
3. After this, add vanilla extract and stir again.
4. Scoop the medium balls from the cream cheese mixture.
5. Mix up together the almond flour and all the remaining Erythritol.
6. Then coat every cheesecake ball into the almond flour mixture.
7. Freeze the balls for 20 min or until they are solid.
8. Place the cheesecake balls in the Ninja Foodi basket and lower the air fryer lid.
9. Cook the dessert at 400 F for 4 min.
10. When the time is over – serve the dessert immediately.
11. Taste it!

Nutrition value/serving: calories 139, fat 13.1, fiber 0.8, carbs 2.3, protein 3.2

Coconut Pie

Prep time: 6 min, Cooking time: 10 min, Serves: 4

Ingredients

- 1 tablespoon coconut flour
- 5 oz coconut, shredded
- ½ teaspoon vanilla extract
- 1 tablespoon Truvia

- 1 teaspoon butter
- 1 egg, whisked
- ¼ cup heavy cream

Directions

1. Mix up together the coconut flour, coconut shred, and butter.
2. Stir the mixture until homogenous.
3. Add whisked egg, vanilla extract, Truvia, and heavy cream. Stir well.
4. Transfer the pie mixture into the basket and lower the air fryer lid.
5. Set the Bake mode 355F.
6. Cook the pie for 10 min.
7. Check if the pie is cooked with the help of the toothpick and chill it till the room temperature.
8. Serve it!

Nutrition value/serving: calories 185, fat 16.9, fiber 3.9, carbs 8.2, protein 3

Blackberry Cake

Prep time: 8 min, Cooking time: 25 min, Serves: 4

Ingredients

- 4 tablespoons butter
- 3 tablespoon Erythritol
- 2 eggs, whisked
- ½ teaspoon vanilla extract
- 1 oz blackberries
- 1 cup almond flour
- ½ teaspoon baking powder

Directions

1. Combine together all the liquid ingredients.
2. Then add baking powder, almond flour, and Erythritol.
3. Stir the mixture until smooth.
4. Add blackberries and stir the batter gently with the help of the spoon.
5. Take the non-sticky springform pan and transfer the batter inside.
6. Place the springform pan in the pot and lower the air fryer lid.
7. Cook the cake for 20 min at 365 F.
8. When the time is over – check the doneness of the cake with the help of the toothpick and cook for 5 min more if needed.
9. Chill it little and serve!

Nutrition value/serving: calories 173, fat 16.7, fiber 1.1, carbs 2.2, protein 4.2

Raspberry Dump Cake

Prep time: 10 min, Cooking time: 30 min, Serves: 10

Ingredients

- 1 ½ cup coconut flour
- 1 teaspoon baking powder
- 1 teaspoon lemon juice
- ½ cup raspberries
- ¼ cup Erythritol
- 1 egg, whisked
- 1/3 cup almond milk
- 1 tablespoon butter, melted
- ½ teaspoon vanilla extract

Directions

1. Combine together all the dry ingredients.
2. Then add egg, almond milk, and butter.
3. Add vanilla extract and lemon juice.
4. Stir the mixture well. You have to get a liquid batter.
5. Place the layer of the raspberries in the silicone mold.
6. Pour batter over the raspberries.
7. Place the mold on the rack and insert it into Ninja Foodi basket.
8. Close the air fryer lid and set Bake mode.
9. Cook the cake for 30 min at 350 F.
10. When the cake is cooked – chill it well.
11. Turn upside down and transfer on the serving plate.
12. Enjoy!

Nutrition value/serving: calories 107, fat 4.5, fiber 8.9, carbs 15.1, protein 4.3

Vanilla Custard

Prep time: 5 min, Cooking time: 10 min, Serves: 4

Ingredients

- 3 egg yolks
- 1 cup almond milk
- 1 teaspoon vanilla extract
- 2 tablespoon Truvia

Directions
1. Whisk together egg yolk and Truvia.
2. Add vanilla extract and almond milk.
3. Preheat Ninja Foodi at Sauté/Stear mode at 365F for 5 min
4. Then pour the almond milk mixture and Sauté it for 10 min.
5. Stir the liquid all the time.
6. When the liquid start to be thick – transfer it into the serving jars and leave it for 1 hour in the fridge.
7. Serve it!

Nutrition value/serving: calories 181, fat 17.7, fiber 1.3, carbs 6.2, protein 3.4

Peanut Butter Cookies

Prep time: 10 min, Cooking time: 11 min, Serves: 7

Ingredients
- 1 tablespoon Truvia
- 1 egg, whisked
- 6 oz cashew butter

Directions
1. Mix up together all the ingredients and make the small balls.
2. Place the balls in the basket of Ninja Foodi and close the lid.
3. Set the Bake mode and cook the cookies at 330 F for 11 min.
4. Increase the time of cooking if you like crunchy cookies.
5. Serve!

Nutrition value/serving: calories 152, fat 12.6, fiber 0.5, carbs 7.4, protein 5.1

Tender Pudding

Prep time: 10 min, Cooking time: 25 min, Serves: 4

Ingredients
- 3 eggs, whisked
- ½ teaspoon vanilla extract
- 4 tablespoons pumpkin puree
- 1 teaspoon pumpkin pie spices
- 1 cup heavy cream
- 2 tablespoon Erythritol
- 1 cup water, for cooking

Directions
1. Whisk together the eggs, vanilla extract, pumpkin puree, pumpkin pie spices, cream, and Erythritol.
2. Pour the liquid into the non-sticky cake pan.
3. Pour water in the pot.
4. Place the pudding in a cake pan in the pot on the rack and close the lid.
5. Select Steam mode and cook the dessert for 25 min.
6. Let the cooked pudding rest for 10 min (open Foodi lid).
7. Place it in the fridge for a minimum of 4 hours.
8. Enjoy!

Nutrition value/serving: calories 159, fat 14.5, fiber 0.5, carbs 2.7, protein 5

Almond Bites

Prep time: 10 min, Cooking time: 14 min, Serves: 5

Ingredients
- 1 egg, whisked
- 1 cup almond flour
- ¼ cup almond milk
- 1 tablespoon coconut flakes
- ½ teaspoon vanilla extract
- ½ teaspoon baking powder
- ½ teaspoon apple cider vinegar
- 2 tablespoons butter

Directions
1. Mix up together the whisked egg, almond milk, apple cider vinegar, baking powder, vanilla extract, and butter.
2. Stir the mixture and add almond flour and coconut flakes. Knead the dough.
3. If the dough is sticky – add more almond flour.
4. Make the medium balls from the dough and place them on the rack of Ninja Foodi.
5. Press them gently with the hand palm.
6. Lower the air fryer lid and cook the dessert for 12 min at 360 F.
7. Check if the dessert is cooked – and cook for 2 min more for a crunchy crust.
8. Enjoy!

Nutrition value/serving: calories 118, fat 11.5, fiber 1, carbs 2.4, protein 2.7

www.ingramcontent.com/pod-product-compliance
Lightning Source LLC
Chambersburg PA
CBHW080610170426
43209CB00007B/1388